The Dyslexia-Friendly Primary School

A Practical Guide for Teachers

The Dyslexia-Friendly Primary School

A Practical Guide for Teachers

Barbara Pavey

Paul Chapman Publishing

Paul Chapman Publishing
A SAGE Publications Company
1 Oliver's Yard
55 City Road
London EC1Y 1SP

SAGE Publications Inc
2455 Teller Road
Thousand Oaks, California 91320

SAGE Publications India Pvt Ltd
B 1/I 1 Mohan Cooperative Industrial Area
Mathura Road, Post Bag 7
New Delhi 110 044

SAGE Publications Asia-Pacific Pte Ltd
33 Pekin Street #02-01
Far East Square
Singapore 048763

Library of Congress Control Number: 2007925829

British Library Cataloguing in Publication Data
A catalogue record for this book is available from the British Library

ISBN 978-1-4129-1029-3
ISBN 978-1-4129-1030-9 (pbk)

Typeset by Pantek Arts Ltd, Maidstone, Kent
Printed in Great Britain by Cromwell Press Ltd, Trowbridge, Wiltshire
Printed on paper from sustainable resources

Contents

Photocopiable Resources

List of Figures

Acknowledgements

I would like to thank the people who have encouraged me and helped me with comments. They include Rea Reason, Jean Salt, Paul Lismore, Kate Pearson, Lyn Middleton, Debbie Avington, Sue Sanders, Mike Bottery, and an anonymous reader.

I would like to give particular thanks to Gill Harper-Jones, Educational Psychologist and Lecturer at Swansea University and Swansea Institute of Higher Education, for her contributions and advice; to Andrew Bedford, Finance Director of Rotherham Metropolitan Borough Council; and to Margaret Meehan, dyslexia tutor at Swansea University and independent dyslexia consultant.

With regard to resources, I should mention that the dyslexia-friendly lesson plan was amended and developed from a format by Yvonne Hillier. The Dyslexia Accessibility Guide was developed from a differentiation guide written by Margaret Allen and me in 1993.

Finally, I would like to thank the editorial team at Paul Chapman Publishing, Jude Bowen, Katie Metzler and Charlotte Saunders. I am very grateful for their support and advice, and for their considerable patience.

This book is dedicated to

Ron Pick

Teacher and Friend

About the author

Training originally as a primary teacher, Barbara Pavey later taught visual and performing arts, personal and social education, and English in a variety of educational settings, working also as a special educational needs (SEN) coordinator in a secondary school. She followed this with SEN administrative experience, working first as a statement officer for Doncaster LEA and then as the Education Officer for SEN for North Lincolnshire Council.

Through this range of experience, Barbara has gained a deep understanding of children's learning needs, including the learning needs of children who experience dyslexia, and the strategies we can use to help them. Added to this has been the understanding and appreciation of the views of practitioners and families that inform this book.

Barbara developed her dyslexia interest further while leading the SEN and dyslexia postgraduate programmes at Swansea University. In addition to her other educational and SEN qualifications, she holds a Postgraduate Diploma in SEN/Dyslexia and has AMBDA status.

Barbara nows leads the dyslexia studies programmes at the University of Birmingham.

Map of Book

	Chapter 1	Chapter 2	Chapter 3	Chapter 4	Chapter 5	Chapter 6	Chapter 7	Chapter 8
Title	Developing an Understanding of Dyslexia	A Dyslexia-Friendly Focus	Dyslexia-Friendly Perspectives	The Family View	The Dyslexia-Friendly Initiative and the Local Authority	From the Dyslexia-Friendly Local Authority to the Dyslexia-Friendly School	From the Dyslexia-Friendly School to the Dyslexia-Friendly Classroom	Ways Forward
Content	• Background definitions • The social construction of dyslexia • The present position	• What do we understand about dyslexia? • Taking a dyslexia-friendly view • Theoretical and practical points	• Discussion and evaluation of the initiative • The Quality Mark process • Multicultural issues • Power relationships in schools	• Parents' and families' views • Mismatches in views about dyslexia • Policy issues • Labelling • Partnership working	• Policy, management, assessment • The provision of dyslexia support • Scope for innovation	• Existing measures • How dyslexia-friendly is my school? • Practitioners' experience • Resource implications	• How dyslexia-friendly is my classroom? • Photocopiable resources – Lesson plan – Accessibility guide – Self-evaluation tool	CONCLUSION
Practical section theme	Advantages of developing dyslexia awareness	Refocusing what we know in a dyslexia-friendly way	Supporting the gaining of literacy skills	Developing communications with parents and carers	Making LA policies and provisions more accessible and transparent	Sustaining the dyslexia-friendly approach in schools	Practical aspects of classroom work	
Some practical suggestions	About sending information home	About sequencing and instructions	About in-class support and withdrawal lessons	About school – home reporting	About accessible LA SEN/inclusion websites	About budgetary implications for dyslexia-friendly training	About individual education plans (IEPs)	

Case study	A new girl in class: Lara	A useful outcome using a multisensory method: Jed	Use of a simple technique builds skill and confidence: Janey	Dyslexia- friendly, but not as intended: Sean	A creative use of the specialist teacher's time: Aaron	The revamped spelling test: Marta	The value of observation: Tony
Suggestions for practitioners	Reflect on our own experience to inform us in improving practice	Exploit information and communication technology, drawing, diagramming, in alternative ways of recording work	Think about communication and power relationships, including learning differences when English or Welsh is not a child's first language.	• Rehearse/prepare for communication • Talk to alternative language team • Think of how we would like to be communicated with	Make room for innovation – within school practice, with agreement of the SEN Coordinator (SENCo), and via the IEP	• Signal willingness to take training. • Plan ahead for when dyslexia-friendly trained staff move on	Find time/ opportunity to observe children
Suggestions for parents and carers	Reflect on our own experience to inform us in developing partnerships	• Expect understandable explanations about the use of alternative recording methods • Seek more use of these if a child is disadvantaged by too much traditional recording	Ask the LA about dyslexia-friendly policy, and what it understands by this	Have friends or advocates present for support at meetings about a child's learning needs	Request that LA SEN information be made available on websites that are easy to reach and read and include a helpline access point.	Ask school governors for dyslexia-friendly school policy. If this is not in place, request that governors ask LA about its dyslexia-friendly policies/ intentions	Request that school offers dyslexia-friendly training to parents and carers if interested, so that approaches may be carried over.

	Chapter 1	Chapter 2	Chapter 3	Chapter 4	Chapter 5	Chapter 6	Chapter 7	Chapter 8
You can try	Checking text readability	Letting children do the picture first	Cloze procedure	Paired reading	Getting the Mind Map® Habit	Scrutinising photocopies	Miscue analysis	
Summary: Three points to remember	1 Improve the learning environment to lessen the impact of impairment 2 De-mystify dyslexia, make more accessible to all 3 The dyslexia-friendly approach is of value to all learners	1 A dyslexia-friendly approach is everyone's job 2 Teachers are asked to put their existing knowledge together with dyslexia knowledge. This chapter seeks to show how 3 Children respond to different approaches – it is useful to widen scope	1 The dyslexia-friendly approach is LA-wide, top-down; not just about schools, classrooms 2 The dyslexia-friendly approach is about attitude change 3 It is important not to confuse a specific learning difficulty with an alternative language difficulty. Alternative language specialists can help.	1 Emotional aspects affect families 2 Perceptions of dyslexia differ between professionals 3 Perceptions of dyslexia also differ between professionals and parents	1 The dyslexia-friendly approach can be of value to LAs in many ways 2 There are variations among and between LAs' understanding of 'dyslexia-friendly' 3 There are variations between LAs' assessment and the provision practices of LAs	1 The dyslexia-friendly approach is valued in schools 2 Effort is needed to sustain the dyslexia-friendly approach, including planning ahead 3 There are resource implications, but also scope for new arrangements	1 Although dyslexia-friendly policy starts at the top, there is a lot practitioners can do to make classrooms more supportive 2 The dyslexia-friendly process can be maintained through review 3 Good practice requires listening to children's views, and involving parents and carers	

Introduction

In a book described as 'a practical guide', readers are entitled to expect to find items that will help them in their everyday work, rather than theoretical discourse. I hope I have provided enough practical ideas and experiences to satisfy this expectation. Nevertheless, theory can be valuable, too, because it helps us to choose one strategy over another in seeking to help a child, if we do not have direct experience for a guide. For this reason, this book will include theoretical aspects of dyslexia.

In order to invite readers to take what they want from the book, the chapters are laid out in two parts. In Chapters 1–7, the first part of each is discursive, and the second practical. The practical sections comprise a selection of pointers grouped more or less around a central theme. Included in the practical sections are suggestions for practitioners and suggestions for parents and carers. It is hoped too that the discussion and practical points will be of value to local authority (LA) planners and administrators.

Therefore, Chapter 1 provides an overview of what is currently understood about dyslexia, and Chapter 2 casts this knowledge within a socially mediated, dyslexia-friendly context. It includes good practice points. Chapter 3 describes the dyslexia-friendly initiative and the Quality Mark measures, together with multicultural aspects and a consideration of power relationships in schools. Chapter 4 provides the family view. Chapter 5 looks at what the dyslexia-friendly initiative means for LAs, while Chapter 6 moves the focus to the school, and includes the experience of practitioners engaged in the dyslexia-friendly process. Chapter 7 considers the dyslexia-friendly approach in the classroom, and includes planning, guidance and evaluation resources for practitioners. Chapter 8 provides concluding thoughts and considers ways forward.

Nearly 20 years of the National Curriculum has accompanied something of a schism in the teaching and learning of literacy. While the National Literacy Strategy works for many children, its technicist approach has coincided with the development of a separate, different body of knowledge in support of children who have significant literacy difficulties and who have been identified as experiencing dyslexia. In the period since the National Curriculum became the focus of learning, dyslexia research and knowledge have been developing, and to some extent this has created a separate career strand for practitioners.

The dyslexia-friendly initiative now provides an approach that supports and blends both the mainstream and the specialist knowledge domains. It moves dyslexia knowledge into the realm of regular mainstream practice, in the interests of children who experience significant difficulties in gaining literacy skills. This knowledge works in the interests of others too. The dyslexia-friendly initiative takes the view that what is good teaching for children experiencing dyslexia is likely to be beneficial to learners generally.

Most of the ideas in this book are not deeply specialised, although it is hoped that they are insightful. Many are ideas that used to be thought of as practitioners' 'craft knowledge'. Practitioners often describe feeling that they lack training to meet inclusion needs in the classroom. I hope that in refocusing upon aspects of dyslexia and literacy craft knowledge, this book will aid practitioners in developing further confidence. It is important that practitioners believe that they can make a difference when children experience dyslexia, and to appreciate that they have craft knowledge to call upon for this purpose.

I would like to add a note about terminology. The medical model is difficult to dislodge from ideas about special educational needs (SEN), learning difficulties and/or disabilities, or inclusion. We might be used to discussing a child in terms of symptoms, diagnosis, treatment, or co-morbidity, and believe, because this is usual practice, that it is satisfactory practice. This book, however, follows different principles, those of the social model of disability, which seeks to remove barriers to social access, and indeed learning, that are raised by the practice of speaking of people in medicalised terms, or describing them in terms of their impairment. This includes the avoidance of 'othering' children by describing them as dyslexics, or saying that they 'have' dyslexia as if it were an illness.

The social model of disability also requires that people with the difficulties under discussion are also part of that discussion, and that their experience is valued as an important part, if not the most important part, of the discourse. In respecting this view, I am grateful for the advice and support of colleagues who experience dyslexia for themselves.

1

Developing an Understanding of Dyslexia

This chapter sets the scene for a discussion covering the development of our present understanding of dyslexia. It tells you about:

- the background of our understanding of dyslexia

- definitions, research trends and the present position

- the social construction of dyslexia, the social model of disability, and the development of the dyslexia-friendly turn of thinking

- principles and practices related to dyslexia awareness.

A medium-sized primary school might have around 300 pupils, of whom, according to current perceptions, about 30 will experience dyslexia, although they may have different learning characteristics within that experience. Around 12 of the 30 children will experience dyslexia to the extent that it interferes considerably with their learning.

In the primary school, this is likely to appear as a difficulty in gaining basic literacy skills, and a linked difficulty in producing written work. Some children will be non-readers or reading at an elementary level; others may have gained reasonable reading skills but be struggling with spelling. A few may have neat handwriting, while the work of others may be distinctly scruffy and a matter of despair to teachers, parents and, perhaps, to the children themselves. Certain children will keep a low profile while one or two will be angry and unhappy. Some will seem clumsy and disorganised, while others will seem super-organised yet somehow unable to produce the level of work of which their teachers think they are capable.

A number of children will already have been identified as experiencing dyslexia and may receive a certain amount of extra tuition and additional support in class, possibly provided through a statement of special educational needs (SEN). Additionally there will be children who may have been identified as 'at risk' of developing dyslexic-type difficulties, depending on whether they have undergone a screening process or, perhaps, on whether they have close relatives who also experience dyslexia.

Sadly, a minority of children may not have their difficulties recognised until a later stage in their education. There is a number of reasons why this might be the case. Children may appear to be reading at an appropriate level for their age, when, intellectually, they have much more to offer so that their relative difficulty is not recognised. Alternatively, a particular literacy difficulty may just be seen as one weak skill among a number of weak skills demonstrated by a child described as experiencing moderate learning difficulties, and its significance may not be identified. Sometimes literacy difficulties will not become apparent until a later stage when the work level becomes harder. For other children, dyslexia may not be considered when they develop reading skills but continue to have difficulty with spelling or written expression.

A number of the children experiencing dyslexia in primary school are likely to start becoming aware at an early age that literacy work for others seems to be easy, while for them it is difficult, tiring, and defeating. Within the school, in spite of any efforts on the part of the staff to be even-handed and avoid ascribing blame, every child will have an exact knowledge of where they are in the 'pecking order' of readers in their class, and be aware of their own consequent social status within the class. They will perhaps perceive themselves to be at the bottom of the heap, possibly carrying that thought with them throughout their educational lives, until they can leave and find their own way forward, and even then the difficulty will remain. Just as there is a range of difficulty among children experiencing dyslexia, so there will be a range of responses, which must surely be linked to the awareness and responses of the adults around them. The ones who manage most successfully will, in their young lives, find the patience to keep trying and to work harder to reach a similar standard of outcome to their peers.

A dyslexia-friendly turn of thinking

If they are lucky, the children described above will find themselves in the care of practitioners who understand something of the characteristics of dyslexia, and who make corresponding adjustments within teaching and learning. This basic facilitating ethos is one of the central tenets of the dyslexia-friendly approach that is gaining ground in schools today. The term 'dyslexia-friendly' sounds as though it means being sympathetic to children and adults who experience dyslexia, but it means far more than this. Indeed, it reflects the latest development in efforts to understand and provide for dyslexia and to help children who experience it.

The dyslexia-friendly approach involves building on what is known about dyslexia to date and applying that knowledge in the regular classroom, in day-to-day teaching, on the grounds that what benefits children with dyslexia, benefits all children. In addition, it requires a commitment by schools to acknowledge, respect and support dyslexia by including among the staff at least one person who is trained in dyslexia and who will disseminate this knowledge to other staff members. It includes an expectation that all school members, including governors and ancillary staff, will support this approach and monitor it to improve their performance in the characteristics of a dyslexia-friendly school.

This book is about the dyslexia-friendly initiative, and its scope for helping children experiencing dyslexia in primary schools. Its purpose is not to attempt to 'skill up' classroom teachers to become dyslexia specialists, or to add in any major way to the workload that teachers already carry. Instead, its purpose is to contribute to a change of approach that will enable teachers to feel empowered rather than to feel that such work is the province of the Special Educational

Needs Coordinator (SENCo), specialist teachers, or trained teaching assistants. It takes this approach in the belief that practices that help children experiencing dyslexia will help other children with disabilities and learning needs, and will also help those who do not have disabilities and learning needs.

For the purpose of this book, the focus is upon the primary school. Perceptions of dyslexia are explored, tracing the processes leading to the dyslexia-friendly initiative, and considering the questions that arise along the way. It is intended to clarify the present position in ways that support parents and carers, practitioners, and children, and to offer them strategies for the improvement of provision. The practical guidance draws on the dyslexia-friendly initiative, with its aim of maximising potential in an educational climate where reading is seen to be of increasingly fundamental importance, and where anxieties about reading can make headlines.

Background: a developing understanding

Dyslexia can be something of a sensitive subject in the UK. There is a great deal of information now available about dyslexia, yet at the same time there can be confusion resulting from policies, provisions and practices. It is perhaps time that the understanding of dyslexia should spread further than the realm of the specialist, and should become part of the knowledge and skills of the regular class teacher, a view maintained by Gavin Reid (2005a), who has probably written the most about dyslexia.

Nevertheless, dyslexia remains controversial. Some local authorities and some educational psychologists do not use the term, preferring to focus on how to help children rather than label them. Some sources feel that reading difficulty is linked to obstructive teaching approaches, and believe that the National Literacy Strategy is unhelpful to children. Others point out that children who experience difficulty with literacy have less rehearsal of reading, writing and spelling skills simply because literacy activities take them longer. The process is more frustrating and is therefore less rewarding for them, so that difficulties are reinforced. However, although the concept of dyslexia continues to be challenged at times, it has become increasingly accepted as a factor in children's educational progress, and an aspect of learning which must be addressed if a school wishes to consider itself inclusive.

The process of understanding dyslexia has developed since its investigation began toward the end of the nineteenth century. There was a growth of understanding about a particular learning difficulty in the area of literacy that did not seem to be linked to brain injury, and that then came to be known as developmental dyslexia, to distinguish it from the acquired condition that resulted from brain trauma (Thomson, 1985). Since then, dyslexia has been the subject of continuing investigation as to how it might be identified, and how children and adults experiencing dyslexia might be helped.

For some time, then, dyslexia was understood in terms of an inability to gain reading skills, although some did not accept that there was any such difficulty, linking it with laziness, disaffection, or lack of practice. The general understanding of dyslexia seemed to be that it was characterised by a child of above average ability, who inexplicably could not grasp the skills of reading, no matter how hard he tried – the difficulty was usually seen as the problem of boys. However, some commentators saw dyslexia as a way of describing reading or other educational failure in terms found acceptable by the middle classes when explaining, and seeking help for, their own children's learning difficulties (Tomlinson, 2001).

During the latter part of the twentieth century, dyslexia enquiry became established as a significant area of educational research, development and expertise. Dyslexia interest groups specialised in developing training, publications, research and representation, providing a valuable resource for parents and practitioners. This interest in dyslexia continues, gaining an international dimension, as researchers explore the context of different language and graphic systems.

Increasing understanding of the learning characteristics described by the term 'dyslexia' shows that they are not confined to class, gender or cultural groups. Many families can describe older family members who had difficulty in gaining literacy skills, and who consequently were thought of as lacking intelligence. In present-day terms, with dyslexia in mind, their learning difficulties might be considered differently. Today, although dissenting voices may still be heard, for the most part, dyslexia is accepted as a significant learning characteristic experienced by a number of children and adults.

Defining dyslexia

There are many definitions of dyslexia. One of the most widely-used current definitions comes from the British Psychological Society:

> Dyslexia is evident when accurate and fluent word reading and/or spelling develops very incompletely or with great difficulty. This focuses on literacy learning at the 'word level' and implies that the problem is severe and persistent despite appropri-ate learning opportunities. It provides the basis for a staged process of assessment through teaching. (British Psychological Society, 1999: 20)

This definition emphasises a difficulty that does not respond to regular learning interventions, but it does not explain what is meant by 'appropriate learning opportunities', nor whether these refer to learning within the regular classroom or to learning by means of individual tuition.

> Another widely used definition is from the British Dyslexia Association:

> Dyslexia is a combination of abilities and difficulties that affect the learning process in one or more of reading, spelling and writing. It is a persistent condition. Accompanying weaknesses may be identified in areas of speed processing, short-term memory, sequencing, spoken language and motor skills. There may be difficulties with auditory and/or visual perception. It is particularly related to mas-tering and using written language, which may include alphabetic, numerical and musical notation (BDA website).

This definition is more descriptive and, in addition to identifying difficulties, goes on to focus on strengths such as the creativity or practical skills that may be part of the learning style of a child who experiences dyslexia. While definitions so far have taken a within-child view, increasingly there are changing perspectives which focus less on dyslexia as a deficit.

Dyslexia and research

At present, there is a considerable research focus upon brain configuration, phonological processing, and genetics in dyslexia. Just as research into differences in brain characteristics supports the legitimacy of dyslexia, so, too, does genetic research. Dyslexia is currently being linked with around 13 genes (Tolmie, 2006), and the enquiry continues. Twin studies confirm that dyslexia is approximately 50 per cent the result of genetic factors and about 50 per cent the result of environmental ones (Stein, 2004).

There has also been considerable interest in the relationship between diet and dyslexia. This tends to focus on the value of supplementing highly unsaturated fatty acids, linking these to the development of the nervous system. It is considered that supplementing diet with fish oils can improve functioning in literacy and can help pupils who experience other particular learning difficulties that may be linked with dyslexia (Cyhlarova et al., 2004; Richardson et al., 2004).

For classroom practitioners, and for parents and carers, the value of research lies in the knowledge it can contribute to ways to improve the learning environment, and in the legitimacy conferred by the scientific view. If dyslexia is only about 50 per cent likely to be the result of genetic factors, then there is a good level of potential impact for the learning environment in the other 50 per cent. This encourages practitioners to believe that what they do can make a real difference.

Morton and Frith's frequently described three-stage causal model (Morton and Frith, 1995, cited by the Working Party of the Division of Educational and Child Psychology of the British Psychological Society, 1999) has become widely acknowledged because it brings together the different approaches to understanding dyslexia. The model shows dyslexia to be considered in three related ways; in terms of the brain or biology, that is, the linkages or anomalies in the brain structure, and the contribution of genetics; in terms of cognition, that is, the thinking process; and in terms of behaviour, that is, the things that children do when tackling the process of gaining skills in reading, writing and spelling, and mathematics. Alongside all three elements runs the recognition that environment, including the learning environment, is a factor.

A dyslexia-friendly focus upon the three-level causal model acknowledges that while there are different ways of viewing dyslexia, all three suggested elements (brain processes, thinking processes and learning behaviour) are affected by environmental factors. This indicates that greater attention paid to the learning environment can have an impact upon the other elements. Such an approach matches current perspectives that move away from traditional deficit-based or medically-based views and toward a more socially mediated view of disability.

The present position

In contrast to earlier perspectives, a social model of disability is gaining in importance. The social model embodies the principle that while an individual may have impairments, it is society, that is, the social context, that disables. This stands in contrast to a medical model, which interprets disability in terms of a medical difficulty with a medical solution, and a deficit-based model which places the focus squarely upon the individual, discussing disability in terms of his or her perceived shortcomings. While it also has its critics, the social model perspective is gaining in importance, and is the basis for the position taken in the highly influential Index for Inclusion (Booth and Ainscow, 2002). Taking a social context view suggests possibilities for improving learning by improving the learning environment, and this is at the heart of both the Inclusion Index and the dyslexia-friendly initiative.

Barbara Riddick (2001) describes how the Warnock Report (DES, 1978) and the resulting 1981 Education Act took a social model perspective on SEN. These landmark events removed categorisation, replacing it with the principle of making learning accessible to children by tailoring resources to their learning needs. Educational legislation since then has directed policy for children with learning difficulties toward a more context-based view, particularly since 1997, when a change of government began supporting a more socially oriented and inclusive approach.

Government education policies and guidance generally acknowledge dyslexia, although not always using that particular term. The Primary National Strategy refers to children who have difficulty in gaining literacy skills, describing help for their learning needs in terms of three waves of intervention, increasing in intensity. The first wave is represented by the National Literacy Strategy, and the second by catch-up programmes and interventions that may be put in place by the school, but which are not necessarily seen as indicating that children experience SEN. The third wave involves focused interventions, involving specialist advice. To support these interventions, the Department for Education and Skills (DfES) has produced a CD-ROM, *Learning and Teaching for Dyslexic Children* (DfES, 2005).

The SEN codes of practice for England and Wales both place dyslexia within the context of cognition and learning, which includes general and specific learning difficulties and their associated learning needs ([DfES, 2001; National Assembly for Wales, 2002]; in both codes, this information is found in Chapter 7, paragraphs 7: 58/59). Within the codes, children experiencing specific learning difficulties, including dyslexia, developmental coordination disorder (dyspraxia), dyscalculia and other related difficulties, are identified as a separate group from children experiencing moderate, severe or profound general learning difficulties, although the codes acknowledge the potential for overlap.

The position of the codes brings some form of resolution to the earlier debate about whether dyslexia should or should not be described as a specific learning difficulty. The debate centred on whether dyslexia is seen in relation to particular cognitive characteristics, or whether it is identified in terms of a discrepancy, usually with an expected intelligence level. The terms are generally now used interchangeably, with a reference to literacy distinguishing this particular difficulty from others.

In spite of inclusive perspectives, a focus on labelling and categorisation continues. In the school context, this can be seen in the collection of Pupil Level Annual School Census (PLASC) data. This contains 12 categories, and dyslexia would fall within the category of 'specific learning difficulties'. It seems as if the government seeks to satisfy contradictory perspectives. On the one hand, it is identifying and counting pupils with specific learning difficulties, including dyslexia, suggesting an individual-deficit view. On the other hand, the SEN codes of practice and current policies support the view that social and environment factors are crucially important. Such tensions are not unusual within discussions of SEN and dyslexia provision.

The SEN codes of practice are careful to consider all factors. In discussing children who might need statutory assessment for a statement of SEN, they focus on levels of attainment, but are also concerned that rate of progress and style of progress should also be considered. The codes cover all bases by pointing out that attainment should be considered in line with what is understood or expected of a child's ability, suggesting a discrepancy model, at the same time acknowledging that a child so identified would have difficulties that are exceptionally complex and entrenched. This relates to views of dyslexia as an unexpected difficulty that does not respond to regular teaching approaches. In addition, the codes embrace something of the social model in their view that, among other possible external factors, school organisation, rather than any inherent learning difficulty or disability, may result in a child's reduced performance. It is such factors of school organisation that a dyslexia-friendly approach seeks to address.

The social construction of dyslexia

There is a growing interest in the ways in which dyslexia may be said to be socially constructed; put simply, this says that what we understand about dyslexia is shaped by social expectations, discourse and requirements. Kevin Woods (1998) has pointed out the extent to which the discussion of dyslexia has fallen within the area of cognitive psychology, calling this 'narrow'. He feels that it would be helpful to examine the different perceptions of dyslexia, to build a definition of dyslexia that includes broader social understandings. Ruth Paradice (2001) continues this theme, focusing on the ways in which parents, educational psychologists and SENCOs view dyslexia. She points out that the term 'dyslexia' has passed into common usage to describe children who have difficulty in gaining literacy skills. As a term, 'dyslexia' has acquired everyday meanings that exist in social contexts and that coexist with professional and technological meanings.

An understanding of dyslexia as having a complex social identity links with ideas about a social model of disability. Barbara Riddick (2001) develops this point when she confirms that dyslexia has become a cause for concern because of the increasing demand for general literacy in the population, and because of the resulting disadvantages and social consequences of illiteracy. In a society differently oriented, dyslexia would not generate the same problems.

Dyslexia is defined as a disability under the Disability Discrimination Act 1995 when the impairment has 'a substantial and long term effect on a person's ability to carry out normal day to day activities'. This makes it appropriate to consider the social model of disability in thinking about dyslexia, and to consider how the social environment can be improved to help people experiencing this difficulty, however it may be understood or defined. For children in school, the dyslexia-friendly initiative represents a concerted effort to move support and effective action into the realm of the learning environment and away from the 'narrow' perspective of cognitive impairment, with its focus upon child deficit.

Principles and practices

The suggestions in this section reflect the general theme of the advantages of developing dyslexia awareness.

Some practical points about sending information home

- Schools need to send information home, and the usual form of information-sharing is a letter. A child experiencing dyslexia is likely to have trouble in making the transfer without difficulty. This piece of paper may look like many others, and its content or significance may not be obvious. It may get mixed up with another similar-looking paper. A child experiencing dyslexia may experience organisational difficulties and misplace the letter, or experience memory difficulties and forget about the letter.

- When it arrives at home, parents or carers who also experience dyslexia may then meet a similar range of obstacles in coping with the letter, and all this may prevent the information from reaching its target.

- It is also possible that a letter of this kind would be computer generated, or written from a template. Even if the letter was written personally, dyslexia accessibility might not have been a consideration.

- With all this potential difficulty, it would be practical for school practitioners to share information with families and carers in accessible formats that keep letters and letter content to a minimum, or in formats that make use of modern technology. It would help to indicate clearly when a response is required. Where letters have to be used, they can be made more accessible by following the readability process below, and the text resource guide in Chapter 7.

A case study that reflects the improved relationships resulting from a dyslexia-friendly approach when someone new enters the class

Case Study

Lara

Mrs B had moved into the area with her 10-year-old daughter Lara, and had approached the local primary school about enrolling her. At first, Mrs B was ready for an argument, because at the last school she had experienced difficulty in getting recognition for Lara's learning needs, as she understood them. At that school Lara was eventually tested for literacy problems by the SENCo, and the possibility was raised of dyslexic-type difficulties. The process of referral in that LA meant that she would be referred to the educational psychologist and the central support team. From then on, Lara sometimes received support in class from a learning support assistant, but, essentially, Mrs B felt that Lara did not get sufficient help, and the answer to her question as to whether Lara was dyslexic seemed to have been put on hold until the educational psychologist could assess her.

Mrs B was relieved to find a different reception at the new school. The first difference was that staff did not seem to see Mrs B as a 'fussy mum' or want to avoid discussing Lara's learning needs in terms of dyslexia. The next difference was that they did not see the responsibility for understanding Lara's learning needs and providing for them as belonging to an expert outside the school. Finally, the school had a number of approaches and processes in place that were designed to help children with dyslexia, and these were explained to Mrs B and discussed with her. Mrs B was able to describe the things that she felt helped Lara to learn, as was Lara herself. Mrs B came away heartened. She still felt that she would be keeping a close eye on the school to make sure they met Lara's needs, but for now she felt more confident.

A suggestion for practitioners: reflecting on our own experience and improving practice

As practitioners, we could usefully think back to what it was like when we were children in primary school. Was there something we could not do, no matter how hard we tried, such as climb a rope, sing in tune, understand fractions, or spell? If we recall what that was like, we may remember despair, dread, a sinking feeling in the stomach, and a sense of release when it was over and could be left behind, only to have to face it all again the next day. We might recall pupils who could not get on with literacy learning however hard they tried. Or we might remember that everyone seemed to know who the best reader was and who the worst reader in the class, with teachers making this a source of public praise or humiliation. These are all valuable experiences, because they serve as a reminder of what children experiencing dyslexia-type difficulties feel like a lot of the time. We can resolve that the learning experiences that we provide for children are better than those negative ones and take heart from the fact that educational understanding about dyslexia has made progress.

A suggestion for parents and carers: reflecting on our own experience and developing partnerships

As parents and carers, we might also think back to those earlier school days, and about the positive and negative experiences we had. For parents and carers who experienced dyslexia themselves at a time when perhaps it was not recognised, and who experienced blame, struggle and sometimes punishment, those memories might be vivid but not happy ones. But for parents and carers as well as practitioners, there is value in what we can learn from that experience, and the resolutions we make that things are going to be different for our children. The beginning of making that learning experience better lies in our partnership with schools. Dyslexia is a slippery concept about which there remains much discussion. Uncertainty about how it is defined, managed and supported may spill over into schools. Nevertheless, we, as parents and carers, can be confident about our right to have our children's needs met in school. We can expect to have a proper discussion of dyslexia. We are entitled to expect a reasonable answer to the question, 'What are you going to do to help my child?' If a child has an educational need, the answer in the present-day UK cannot ever be 'nothing'.

You can try

A technique to enhance learning for children experiencing dyslexia: checking text readability

Text readability

There is a tool in the Word computer program that can be used to improve the readability of text. After loading Word, go to:

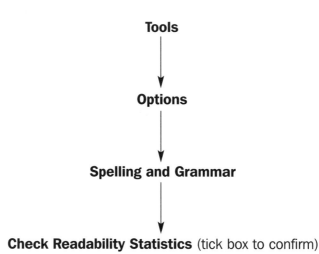

Tools

↓

Options

↓

Spelling and Grammar

↓

Check Readability Statistics (tick box to confirm)

Then close this screen and type the text as a normal Word document.

When you have finished, run the spellchecker.

On completion, the screen will display the readability statistics. You should:

- Aim for the lowest possible percentage of passive sentences.

- Aim for the highest possible measure of 'Flesch Reading Ease'.

- Aim for the lowest 'Flesch–Kincaid Grade level'; this gives an American grade level.

- Add 5 to the Flesch–Kincaid level to get an approximate reading age.

(With acknowledgements to Yewlands School)

Key Points to Remember

1. Children will be helped by a move away from an individual, deficit-based view, and toward awareness of a social model of learning difficulty and/or disability and its implications. Broadly, the social model takes the position that although people may have impairments, it is society that disables. We can improve the learning environment to lessen the impact of impairment.

2. Children will be helped by demystifying dyslexia and dyslexia specialist teaching. Making dyslexia ideas and techniques more accessible to practitioners and parents, so that they feel more confident about helping children who experience dyslexia, represents recognition of a craft knowledge in the teaching of literacy.

3. One of the valuable aspects of the dyslexia-friendly approach is that it helps children whether or not they experience literacy difficulties described as dyslexia. This is because it is founded on principles that are based on knowledge of helpful practice in teaching and learning.

Further reading

Reid, G., 2003, *Dyslexia, A Practitioner's Handbook* (3rd edn), Chichester, Wiley.

Some useful websites with a dyslexia overview

- A summary of the present position regarding dyslexia, 'A Framework for Understanding Dyslexia', can be found at:
  www.dfes.gov.uk/readwriteplus/understandingdyslexia/
  although this is intended for non-specialist teachers in the post-16 setting.

- The DfES Standards site also discusses dyslexia at:
  www.standards.dfes.gov.uk/primary/publications/inclusion/
  11170961/pns_incl1184-2005 dyslexia_sf1.pdf

- Teachernet, the DfES practitioner information site, has information about dyslexia (use the search term 'dyslexia') at:
  teachernet.gov.uk/wholeschool/sen/
  and
  teachernet.gov.uk/teachingandlearning/

2

A Dyslexia-Friendly Focus

This chapter looks at the current issues in dyslexia from a dyslexia-friendly perspective. It tells you about:

- the key issues in current discussions about dyslexia

- theoretical approaches and practical approaches as they are seen today, including information about experiencing dyslexia, how it is expressed, its impact, and relevant methods of teaching and support

- the changing ways that we think about these issues and ideas when adopting a dyslexia-friendly approach

- good practice points that move the focus toward the learning setting

- practical suggestions relating to aspects that we might already know about helping children to learn, and refocusing them in a dyslexia-friendly way.

A dyslexia-friendly perspective moves the emphasis away from child deficit and toward the changes that could be made in the learning setting to support children experiencing dyslexic-type difficulties. Classroom practice of this kind accords with government support for personalised learning (DfES, 2004). A dyslexia-friendly practitioner may move toward an understanding of learning linked to individual preferences and learning styles, sometimes utilising them, sometimes challenging them. The following section takes theoretical and practical aspects associated with dyslexia and considers them in terms of a dyslexia-friendly, socially mediated perspective. Each section is followed by a good practice point, supporting a dyslexia-friendly approach.

How many children experience dyslexia?

Generally, the literature refers to the number of children experiencing dyslexia as falling at around 10 per cent of the school population, although some sources feel that it may be higher.

Out of this 10 per cent of children, approximately 4 per cent are considered to experience dyslexia to the point where their difficulties are significant. The former Dyslexia Institute (now Dyslexia Action, after combining with the Hornsby International Dyslexia Centre) has estimated the number of children in the UK who experience dyslexia severely at about 375,000.

● **Good Practice Point**: some of the primary school age children experiencing dyslexia will not be identified until they are older, for a number or reasons. Because of this, and because it is a useful principle, skilled practitioners may choose to work on the basis that for every child identified as experiencing dyslexia-type difficulties that they know about, there may well be another one that they do not know about. The simplest way forward is to make dyslexia-friendly provision available for all children.

Is it mostly boys who experience dyslexia?

In the past, it has been the view that dyslexia is more commonly found in boys. However, Stein (2004) does not see a direct link between dyslexia and sex (gender) chromosomes, although other genetic mechanisms may be involved, causing dyslexia to seem more prevalent among boys. He goes on to point out that dyslexia experienced among girls may be under-reported.

● **Good Practice Point**: a skilled practitioner does not make assumptions that only boys experience dyslexia, and, as above, works on the basis that some children may be managing or masking their difficulties. Practitioners can keep their eyes open for girls experiencing dyslexic-type difficulties, as well as boys.

How do children experiencing dyslexia manage their learning?

Adults experiencing dyslexia may describe how they managed their difficulties by copying friends' work or asking their friends for help, and by keeping a low profile in class. In many ways, this represents the development of good coping skills and strategies, good partnership skills, and ways of working that reflect children's interest, participation and involvement rather than their level of literacy skill.

Since dyslexia is a range, some children experiencing dyslexia will manage their difficulties well, although classroom practitioners may not see the hours of extra effort put in or the fatigue this generates. However, even in a technologically-developing learning context, children still need to gain independent literacy skills for themselves, and as children get older the work becomes harder.

● **Good Practice Point**: dyslexia-friendly practitioners, while appreciating (not punishing) the coping skills described here, also need to be alert to how children cope when working on their own. This forms part of the practitioner's learning-environment-based assessment. There may be a difference between work produced with peer support and that produced independently, and this may provide an indicator of difficulty. However, sensitive practitioners do not view informal collaboration as 'cheating'; they understand that in everyday life we all get help where we can, when we feel we need it.

Are there other learning characteristics that might have an impact?

It is increasingly recognised that there are areas of overlap among learning characteristics that may include dyslexia, dyspraxia (also known as developmental coordination disorder (DCD)), autism and Asperger's syndrome, attention deficit disorder with or without hyperactivity, and specific language difficulty. They are seen by some as part of a range of difficulties that have a neurological origin. In medical language, this overlap may be described as 'co-morbidity ', a term which technically defines two illnesses occurring at the same time. However, some feel that describing a learning difficulty in terms of illness is unhelpful, so here the term 'co-occurrence' is used.

Dyspraxia, DCD, or motor coordination difficulty, may be experienced by some children whose principal learning difficulty is in the area of literacy. The main impact then may be upon hand-writing. Co-occurrence of dyslexia and other difficulties may be quite high. John Stein (2004) considers that 50 per cent of people who experience dyslexia also show other characteristics – particularly specific language impairment, dyspraxia, and attention deficit hyperactivity disorder (ADHD). In addition 50 per cent of people experiencing these characteristics also experience dyslexia. It may be that, as our understanding increases, separate definitions become less helpful for some children, and may need to be replaced by an understanding of areas of overlap.

- **Good Practice Point**: practitioners can support overlapping learning difficulties by maximising the quality of the learning setting. This means providing good-quality materials that are easy to use, and providing a range of recording techniques, including computers, so that all children may demonstrate their learning. Practitioners can increase quality by considering detail in the matter of resources, as for instance, by making sure that pencils are not too short to hold comfortably, that there is a choice of writing implements, and that there is a supply of Dycem (a form of non-slip matting material, from https://uk-ssl.com/dycem/store) available for children who need to anchor their work more firmly.

Are there any emotional issues?

Children experiencing learning difficulties may lack confidence as they struggle to master the literacy skills that others around seem to manage more easily. They may feel increasingly unhappy when overtaken in skills by siblings. Parents may find themselves having to work hard with their children to help them to manage their school work, or to practise a specialist programme. Parents may also have experienced similar difficulties themselves and have the spectre of their own problematic school days raised in their efforts to aid their children. All the frustrations and angers that may arise from these situations can be complicated by fatigue and reduced morale. Being bullied because of their difficulties may also be part of children's experience (Scott, 2003).

There is so much scope for negativity in the matter of dyslexia that positives may not at first be obvious. However, one may also consider the pleasure and happiness of mastery, the valuing and appreciation of courage and endurance, and the pride and delight at the other skills and qualities manifested by children who also experience dyslexia. Personal experience suggests that children who overcome the difficulties that dyslexia presents are those who have the patience to keep going, maintaining the practice and the repetition, and the redrafting of work. The capacity to do this surely must be related to the emotional support provided by the adults in a child's life.

- **Good Practice Point**: sometimes children may react to the demands of schooling in unacceptable ways, with aggression or 'acting out'. Dyslexia-friendly practitioners, before making judgements about emotional and behavioural difficulties, observe children carefully to see if they react particularly strongly when faced with a literacy task (so many school tasks are literacy tasks), understanding that the fears, tensions and frustrations generated by such tasks are almost unbearable. A tantrum may be the explosion of such fears and tensions when they reach an intolerable level. Skilled practitioners will check the literacy level of children who are 'acting out', if they will permit it and if the situation has not deteriorated too far. Positive self-evaluation and study skills techniques can be built into the literacy curriculum to help learners develop useful strategies that will help them to sustain their learning. Practitioners can acknowledge efforts made and small successes gained, while being sensitive to the lack of confidence and downright unhappiness that children may experience in trying to gain literacy skills.

What are the theoretical accounts of dyslexia?

The phonological, magnocellular and cerebellar accounts of dyslexia are the three explanations that currently have the highest profile. Justice cannot be done to theoretical perspectives by summing them up in a few lines. However, it might be said that the phonological account is concerned with cognitive pathways linked to the language centres of the brain, the magnocellular account is concerned with visual pathways, and the cerebellar account is concerned with the systems that govern balance and gait. All are concerned with the routes by which information reaches the brain and is processed, and how differences in this information processing can affect the gaining of literacy and other skills.

It now seems that these main theories are moving closer together, as Gavin Reid and Angela Fawcett (2004) suggest, and that a simple, causal relationship is not necessarily the answer. There are links between the magnocellular system and the cerebellum, and between the cerebellum and the language area, and there may also be overlap between difficulties encountered in phonological and magnocellular processing. In addition, there are other theoretical aspects, such as difficulty in speed of processing, that contribute to an understanding of dyslexia.

- **Good Practice Point**: practitioners can help by remembering that some children experience difficulties in aural and phonological processing, but respond more strongly to visual input. Others experience difficulties in visual processing, but respond more strongly to aural and phonological input. Being aware of whether a child learns better visually or aurally can help practitioners become more effective. To this can be added the knowledge that some children respond best to kinaesthetic tasks involving handling, doing, making and other practical activities. Taken together, this knowledge leads practitioners naturally toward a multisensory approach.

More about phonological difficulty

A postmodern view can call upon all the major accounts of dyslexia. However, it is useful to give further attention to the area of phonological difficulty, as it is likely to be the area of functioning where dyslexia is most commonly and clearly manifested. It is seen as part of the learning profile of many children experiencing dyslexia, and is described as a 'key characteristic' (Snowling, 2000: 215). Phonological difficulty, which is knowledge of the sounds that combine to make words, has been an important part of understanding dyslexia since the 1980s. However, not all children with reading difficulties clearly experience phonological impairment, and, as John Stein (2004) points out, its presence may indicate another difficulty, such as a language difficulty.

The building of phonological skills plays an important part in current approaches to literacy, as expressed in phonics-based strategies. For phonological teaching to benefit children described as experiencing dyslexia, Virginia Berninger (2004) considers that it needs to be linked quickly to other aspects of literacy and language learning. John Rack (2004) believes that phonological teaching benefits children more when linked to other reading methods than when used alone. He stresses the need for phonological teaching to be placed within a supportive learning context.

What a phonological difficulty means in practice is that practitioners cannot rely upon a letter or syllable sound to 'stick' or even to be recognised as the same each time it appears. The difficulty may relate to, and be compounded by, memory difficulties that prevent the retrieval of aural or visual patterns. The rhyme of similar spelling patterns may not be recognised, or be transferred from one word to another. Reflecting upon this, practitioners may notice how much literacy teaching includes the expectation that similar elements will be recognised and be automatically carried over in the application to new reading, writing and spelling tasks. Where dyslexia is concerned, however, this can be an area of major difficulty.

- **Good Practice Point**: good practice would be to link phonology-based teaching quickly to other literacy learning while it is still fresh, and to link it with other reading methods, reinforcing phonological knowledge and anchoring it in context. This suggests using multisensory, methods, short 'bursts' of input, and frequent reinforcement, drawing attention to the phonological point made. Happily, this corresponds both to modern approaches to literacy and to specialised dyslexia teaching.

Do coloured lenses and coloured overlays help?

Scotopic Sensitivity Syndrome is the term used to identify the visual processing difficulties caused by light. Sometimes it is referred to as Irlen syndrome or as Meares–Irlen syndrome in recognition that Meares was the first to publish a report of the effects. Scotopic sensitivity syndrome describes the visual input characteristics of people who find that print 'jumps about' or that the contrast of black print on white paper is too strong and causes the print to flash. These effects make reading more difficult and physically uncomfortable, possibly even causing headaches. Not all people with Scotopic Sensitivity Syndrome experience dyslexia, and not all people with dyslexia experience Scotopic Senstivity Syndrome. However, there is the possibility of overlap.

For a long time, Irlen syndrome or Scotopic Sensitivity Syndrome was treated with scepticism, because of its lack of scientific, tested evidence. However, since the 1980s, a scientific basis for scotopic sensitivity has developed, significantly through Arnold Wilkins' exploration of the use of coloured overlays (Fawcett, 2002).

Classroom practitioners become involved in this debate at the point at which it is suggested that transparent, coloured overlays or special tinted lenses may help children experiencing dyslexia. The evidence indicates that these items can help some children in gaining reading skills, sometimes quite significantly. Coloured overlays can aid some children's reading progress even when there is no dyslexia present or suspected.

- **Good Practice Point**: head teachers who have the confidence to improve the learning environment for developing readers by providing coloured overlays for anyone who wants them, and by producing materials on tinted paper rather than on (cheaper) white paper, may find that the investment has positive results for many of their pupils. Coloured or 'intuitive' overlays and assessment kits are available from www.ceriumvistech.com and i.o.o.sales.co.uk. A vision test is recommended for children before the assessment is undertaken.

What do we mean by multi-sensory approaches?

The specialised programmes designed to help children experiencing dyslexia who have not responded to more ordinary teaching methods usually share common characteristics. These include being multisensory, using vision, hearing, touch, and possibly other senses, to bring about learning. Multisensory methods are generally supported throughout the dyslexia literature as the best means of helping children to gain literacy skills.

The dyslexia-friendly focus on multisensory approaches is concerned with method – in other words, input – and requires classroom practitioners to think about the nature of the learning experiences they design, providing something for the ears, the eyes and the hands. Guidance from specialised dyslexia programmes suggests that the methods need to be used together, and quickly, in the pursuit of small units of learning that are linked clearly to other units. This has to be done judiciously to avoid overload, but as with other dyslexia-friendly practices, multisensory processes can benefit more learners than just those experiencing dyslexia. Use of colour can be important in guiding visual attention and focus. It can be used in colour coding, highlighting, and colouring areas of importance (not too brightly) in text or display.

- **Good Practice Point**: skilled practitioners include activities such as constructing, diagramming and drawing as a regular part of literacy learning, rather than using them as treats or rewards or regarding them as immature activities. Dyslexia-friendly practitioners also use such activities as alternative ways for children to record their work.

How important are learning styles?

There is a number of different formulations of learning styles, but perhaps the two most fre-quently mentioned within educational practice are the visual, auditory, kinaesthetic (VAK) categorisation and Gardner's multiple intelligence theory. Neil MacKay believes that the learn-ing environment should include VAK and multiple intelligence opportunities as standard practice, along with opportunities for oracy and multisensory methods. He points out the value for all pupils in doing this, adding,

> Opportunities should be created to encourage learners to operate outside of their learn-ing preferences. Taking them outside their 'comfort zones', in a safe environment, will reveal hidden depths and, perhaps, unexpected weaknesses. (MacKay, 2001: 170)

MacKay points out that classroom practitioners also have personal learning styles, and they can extend themselves, and their pupils can benefit, when they deliberately use styles outside their own 'comfort zone'. An important point here is the security of the learning environment, which needs to be structured to allow pupils to explore their own strengths and weaknesses without negative emotional impact.

- **Good Practice Point**: if practitioners are going to explore the possibilities of using multisensory methods and individual learning styles, they also must be prepared to mark work that is delivered in different formats (MacKay, 2005; see also Chapter 7). It would be best for this to happen within a whole-school marking policy.

How important are repetition and overlearning?

Classroom practitioners are not expected to deliver specialist dyslexia teaching programmes but might like to note the need to teach something over and over again, with variations in approach, before it will 'stick'. Practitioners should not expect the automatic, unconscious understanding that some children may experience in gaining literacy skills. Specialist dyslexia teachers confirm, too, that children experiencing dyslexia may have some days that are better than others for remembering what had previously been learnt. They may speak of 'two steps forward, one step back', and, indeed, on some days, it may seem to be the opposite case. However, it should be noted that some sources affirm results for methods that do not involve repetition and overlearning, instead claiming to bring about a more immediate acquisition of literacy. These methods tend to be considered as controversial.

- **Good Practice Point**: a balance needs to be struck between the security of repetition and the transferring of the learning into a new, more unfamiliar context. Using this knowledge classroom practitioners, who already know the value of praise and reassurance, will be pleased to acknowledge what may seem to be small increments of progress made both in knowledge and confidence. On days when children experiencing dyslexia seem to have mislaid the knowledge they had previously grasped, dyslexia-friendly practitioners will know that this is not a case of laziness or wilfulness, but of one learning characteristic among many.

What use can be made of ICT?

Information and communication technology (ICT), particularly word processing, can be an enormous help for children experiencing dyslexia. ICT helps in producing work that reflects interest, knowledge, content and effort, and its use means that judgement about the work need not be hampered because of presentation.

In addition to providing alternative ways of recoding work that children experiencing dyslexia may value, there is a number of ICT programmes designed to aid the development of literacy skills, often enabling children to work independently. SuccessMaker (www.rm.com), WordShark (www.inclusive.co.uk) and Clicker (www.cricksoft.com) are among the best known of these. Some programmes are more clearly focused on dyslexia, while others have a more general literacy-building purpose. There is a wide range of programmes designed to help children of all ages. They can be enjoyably game-like and give their users immediate feedback about their progress.

ICT also has a role in the assessment of dyslexia, most particularly through the work of Chris Singleton, whose assessment programmes are marketed through the firm of Lucid. The early identification program CoPS is probably the best known of these, but there are also assessment programs for older students.

Finally, for older children experiencing dyslexia, there are mathematics, music and graphic representation programs, which will help children to record their work and to demonstrate what they know without being hampered by literacy or graphic difficulties. Spellcheckers are also sometimes thought of as a useful aid for children experiencing dyslexia. Although these can be an admirable resource, they may be of reduced effectiveness unless their user is able to recognise the correct spelling of a word when it appears.

- **Good Practice Point**: supportive practitioners can show their willingness to accept homework that has been word-processed, and make available printing-out facilities and computers in regular classes. One difficulty in making the most of the dyslexia-friendly potential of ICT is that the use of computers or of game-like literacy programs may be kept as treats or used as rewards. For children experiencing dyslexia, access to a computer can be a lifeline that needs to be routinely available.

Principles and practices

The practical suggestions in this section explore more ways of helping children who experience dyslexia, calling on aspects that we might already know about and refocusing them in a dyslexia-friendly way.

Some suggestions for thinking about sequencing and instructions:

- We know that children who experience dyslexia may also experience sequencing and/or memory difficulties. Sequencing can be taught as a skill, both in terms of frequently-used sequences like alphabets and multiplication tables, and in terms of developing structure, ordering and logic through following pathways and identifying 'next steps'.

- To help children, we should think about our own use of sequences, especially when they are expressed as instructions. An instruction like 'Come in, hang your coat up, sit down and open your books at page 10, and then put your hand up when you're ready' contains seven parts. We can give children a greater chance of success by dividing complex instructions like these into smaller sections.

- We can break up instructions by giving a one- or two-part instruction, then another, and then another, before progressing to three-part instructions. Visual cues can also help. We can count how many parts we have included in our instructions and think about the gestures with which we accompany them.

A case study that reflects an experiment in trying a different multisensory technique

Case Study

Jed

Jed had been working his way successfully through a structured multisensory reading, writing and spelling program when he became stuck on the letter combination 'ation'. His teacher had read something about the Davis® basic symbol mastery method and thought she would like to try it. She provided modelling clay and a board, and asked Jed to think of a word that he knew of that used the 'ation' combination. Jed was very good at rugby, and suggested 'Five Nations'. 'OK,' thought the teacher, 'Rugby means nothing to me but a lot to him so we'll give it a go.'

The teacher invited Jed to make a model of Five Nations rugby, not having any idea how he might do it, and watched as Jed began to model the outlines of a rugby pitch with a full complement of players for both sides, the layout being in correct detail – naturally. There were a lot of players and after a while the teacher began to join in modelling the little figures, mostly in order to speed the process up. 'This can't work,' she thought. 'It takes a lot of time and it'll probably come to nothing.' However, she decided to treat it as an experiment. They chatted together about Jed's rugby as he modelled the little figures and put them in place. Finally, the teacher guided Jed in writing 'Five Nations' in clay 'worms' along the front of the modelled rugby pitch. He surveyed the model with pleasure.

Jed took the board away to show his friends, and when he returned, his teacher asked him to spell 'nation', which he did correctly. 'How about "station"?' she asked. Again, Jed spelled the word perfectly, after a moment's thought. This went on for 'formation', 'information', 'combination', and other words where the first parts of the word were spelled regularly and then had the 'ation' letter group at the end. Jed was astonished and delighted at his own prowess, and his teacher was even more astonished. She continued to be astonished when, a few weeks later, Jed could still spell those and other words as he worked them out. The teacher decided to think about ways that she could use the method more widely in the classroom setting.

The Davis® method is registered and is part of the Davis® training programme. (Davis, R. with Braun, E., 1997, *The Gift of Dyslexia*, London, Souvenir Press)

A suggestion for practitioners: exploit ICT, drawing and diagramming as other ways for children to record their work

We can seek to make ICT available for children who want to use it for the processing and recording of work, but to do this, we may need to put forward a case to budget holders for more ICT. The case is built around facilitating expression, facilitating recording, and the gaining of necessary literacy skills, all of which improve the quality of outcomes for children and for schools. Budget considerations should also include scope for repair, maintenance and replacement. Cursive handwriting still needs to be taught, but there is room for other ways of recording written work in the primary school. The Qualifications and Curriculum Authority (QCA, 2004) supports the use of multimodal texts in the classroom. Because practitioners are good readers and writers by definition, we need to make a conscious effort to use diagrams, pictures, charts and plans in both our input and our pupils' work.

A suggestion for parents and carers: promote the chances for children to show their knowledge when they use other ways of recording their work

The suggestions in this chapter may represent some ideas that seem unusual, such as the idea of letting older children use building and making, drawing, and diagramming activities, as well as written activities, to demonstrate their learning. If we, as parents and carers, are puzzled about the use of alternative methods, we should be able to ask for and receive an explanation. Equally, if we feel that our child is disadvantaged by an exclusive dependence on written work, we should feel able to discuss this also. Literacy is more than reading, writing and spelling; in its wider sense, being literate also includes understanding and making use of information, and being knowledgeable. It will be easier for schools to adopt a wider range of formats for delivering and recording learning if they know that they have the support of parents and carers.

You can try

A simple technique to widen children's scope for showing their knowledge: letting children do the picture first

Doing the picture first

The QCA confirms that it is both possible and valuable to use alternative formats incorporating visuals and text to meet the Writing Assessment Strands. They point out that 'looking only at the words runs the risk of missing a lot of what children know' (QCA, 2004: 5). This is particularly the case for children experiencing dyslexic-type difficulties. Sometimes, doing a picture to go with writing is seen as the easy part, the treat that comes after the real work; yet, for some children, that point is never reached as they struggle to achieve what is thought to be a reasonable amount of writing.

Doing the picture first will help children experiencing difficulty by providing a visual element to write about, aiding them in the organisation of their thoughts. It will also show whether they have understood the underlying concepts behind a particular element of teaching. If there are concerns about how much actual writing is produced, one might reason that there is always going to be a reduced amount of writing when children are experiencing difficulty. Further, whether or not they experience dyslexia, there are some children who are more responsive to the visual channel than to the aural channel and still others for whom visual work provides a chance to shine. They too will benefit.

Key Points to Remember

1. Supporting children experiencing dyslexia can be viewed as everyone's job, not just that of the specialist. In a dyslexia-friendly school, all aspects of the learning experience are taken into account when thinking about helping children who experience dyslexia.

2. The dyslexia-friendly initiative asks practitioners to put their existing skills and knowledge together with experience gained over time as to what makes a good learning environment for children experiencing dyslexia. The chapter tries to answer possible questions about dyslexia in ways that can inform regular classroom practice.

3. Different children respond to different approaches, so it is a good idea to widen the scope of both practitioners' input and children's output. This includes using alternative formats to display knowledge and record work.

Further reading

McKeown, S., 1999, *Dyslexia and ICT – Building on Success*, Coventry, British Educational Communication and Technology Agency (BECTA)

Reid, G. and Fawcett, A. (Eds), 2004, *Dyslexia in Context: Research, Policy and Practice*, London, Whurr Publishers

Snowling, M., 2000, *Dyslexia*, Oxford, Blackwell Publishing

Some useful websites with a focus on Information and Communication Technology

- The British Educational Communications and Technology Agency (BECTA) has a page concerned with specific learning difficulties and ICT. It can be found at: http://schools.becta.org.uk/

- A page with information about how technology can help with phonics can be found at: www.dyslexic.com

- An important commercial supplier of software, hardware and assistive technology is SEMERC. Its web address is: www.semerc.com and its catalogue is available at: www.onestopeducation.co.uk

3

Dyslexia-Friendly Perspectives

This chapter explores the British Dyslexia Association (BDA) dyslexia-friendly initiative in greater depth. It tells you about:

- the origins of the dyslexia-friendly initiative and the route to a dyslexia-friendly approach

- the Swansea experience

- the expectations accompanying the dyslexia-friendly approach

- the dyslexia-friendly Quality Mark process

- evaluation of the Dyslexia-Friendly Schools Initiative

- issues about dyslexia when different first languages and different cultures are involved

- dyslexia and power relationships in schools

- practical suggestions relating to the general gaining of literacy skills when children experience significant literacy difficulties.

The term 'dyslexia-friendly' and its concepts in the school setting were originated by Neil MacKay, a trainer and consultant in dyslexia with a previous background as a senior teacher and SENCo. He developed the concepts underpinning dyslexia-friendly schools at Hawarden School, a mainstream comprehensive school with a dyslexia resource facility in North Wales. He describes how children experiencing dyslexia would leave the school with pass grades in GCSE examinations, the majority having five or more passes at grades A to G (MacKay, 2001).

While some of the Hawarden pupils' success was based upon teaching methodology, it is clear that an approach calling on a whole-school ethos played an important part. In addition, Neil MacKay placed emphasis upon developing confidence and success for pupils experiencing dyslexia. Added to these strategies was a careful use of the flexibility within the school system for supporting pupils experiencing SEN. Neil MacKay went on to co-author the key text *Achieving Dyslexia Friendly Schools* (British Dyslexia Association (BDA), 1999), produced by the BDA and endorsed by the government.

The dyslexia-friendly approach, as it now exists, aims to bring together the elements of methodology, confidence building, flexibility and whole-school ethos, in a complete support structure. This starts with the Local Authority (LA), the school, and its policies and management structures. It continues with the specialist and classroom teachers, the support workers within the school, the parents of children experiencing dyslexia, and the children themselves, mobilising all in the interests of helping learners. The dyslexia-friendly initiative goes beyond individual learning characteristics to encourage the development of a supportive learning environment, with the expectation of positive outcomes for all learners.

What takes the dyslexia-friendly approach further than other programmes, projects and services designed to help children experiencing dyslexia is its insistence upon a holistic approach. This includes support from the top down, reflected in nested policies and practices that are intended to culminate in better outcomes for the pupils, and consequently for schools and LAs.

The Swansea experience

The dyslexia-friendly initiative was introduced by Swansea LA, where it was used as a basis for restructuring the central SEN support for pupils experiencing dyslexia. Swansea had become an LA in its own right following local government reorganisation, and inherited a situation not of its own making, but which it had the responsibility to resolve.

The position is described vividly in the BDA booklet *Achieving Dyslexia Friendly Schools*. It depicts a climate of dissatisfaction in which dyslexia provision was insufficient to meet pupils' perceived learning needs. The result was parental and professional frustration, reflected in a high rate of appeals to the then SEN tribunal (now called the SEN and Disability Tribunal – SENDIST). The tribunal appeals were intended by parents to secure for their children the dyslexia provision that the Authority lacked at that time. However, without the dyslexia expertise in the Authority, the result was waiting lists for specialist teaching, and the likelihood of a distortion of priorities, since the provision that was available would have to be assigned as the SEN tribunal directed. The Authority had little choice but to take a reactive, crisis-management approach to meeting the learning needs of pupils experiencing dyslexia.

The architect of Swansea's reformed identity as a dyslexia-friendly Authority was Cliff Warwick, at the time the SEN adviser for the City and County of Swansea. In *Achieving Dyslexia Friendly Schools* he describes how the effect of dyslexia-friendly policy created a climate for positive literacy learning. This led to literacy improvements among learners generally and also improvements in the overall teaching of literacy. The policy and practice included the expectation that personal learning needs should be taken into account, and a wider range of teaching approaches used. *Achieving Dyslexia Friendly Schools* describes how the Authority put in place:

- awareness-raising training at primary and secondary level;

- accredited training in supporting pupils with dyslexia, linked with continuous professional development and BDA-approved teacher status for teachers, including a BDA-accredited course for learning support assistants and training for SEN governors that included a dyslexia-awareness element;

- guidance, support and training, including ICT and software guidance.

Outcomes were very positive. The results included the raising of confidence in the Authority among both parents and school staff, and a massive drop in statements for dyslexia, and in appeals to the tribunal. When pupils were supported within the school, parents apparently did not feel the need for statements.

Following the success in Swansea, the BDA began a campaign based upon the dyslexia-friendly principles embodied in the booklet *Achieving Dyslexia Friendly Schools*. This was circulated to LAs and is now in its fifth edition, providing a comprehensive manual for anyone interested in improving their dyslexia knowledge and practice. The latest edition includes more recent legislation implications, and the insights of people who experience dyslexia are shared throughout.

Dyslexia-friendly expectations

The dyslexia-friendly perspective takes a whole-school approach, rather than, as previously, being limited to the specialised interest of the SENCo, and to visiting specialists such as educational psychologists and support teachers. In their fully developed form, dyslexia-friendly characteristics are linked with school effectiveness. Dyslexia-friendly approaches should therefore be reflected in governor and senior management commitment. This is demonstrated by inclusion within school policy and preferably in the school development plan.

A whole-school approach to dyslexia that is written into school policy must also be carried through in classroom practice if it is to have meaning and impact. This requires both training and attitudinal change, and *Achieving Dyslexia Friendly Schools* points out the need to overcome scepticism, primarily among teachers.

Rather than reflecting disbelief in the existence of dyslexia, this scepticism may reflect reluctance by an already overloaded profession to take on further responsibilities in the management of learning. To this may be added a lack of some teachers' confidence in their own abilities to make the necessary changes, which may be expressed as a need for knowledge and relevant training. Other complicating factors include a long-standing view of dyslexia as the province of specialists, and consequently as the business of specialist units and schools. Set against these factors is the prevailing ethos of inclusion.

Provision of training is one of the cornerstones of the dyslexia-friendly initiative. This carries resource implications. It is noticeable that in the original Swansea initiative this responsibility was taken by the authority, not only as part of its overall school effectiveness strategy, but also in releasing resources that were overstretched in the first instance and then bound into statements. A further aim was to reduce the poor relationships and extensive claims on time that resulted from a high level of appeals to the SEN tribunal.

The intentions and the effect of the Swansea training programme were to equip a sufficient number of teachers with dyslexia expertise to enable one teacher to be within the staff of each school. For some this might have seemed satisfactory provision in itself. However, the dyslexia-friendly initiative further requires that specialism does not remain the province of appropriately trained teachers. It should be passed on to the other members of the school community. The fully developed form of the dyslexia-friendly approach is embodied in the Quality Mark process, which provides an important part of the initiative.

The dyslexia-friendly Quality Mark

The Quality Mark protocol is designed to follow a cumulative process by which an LA can develop and maintain its dyslexia-friendly characteristics. The authority is then endorsed by the BDA as being recognisably and firmly, dyslexia-friendly.

There is a fee attached to this process, and following registration, the Authority has two years to achieve the BDA Quality Mark. Registration is valid for three years, after which renewal must be sought. The registering LA receives a copy of the dyslexia-friendly standards, details of the requirements for the supporting record of evidence, and exemplary school standards. The areas covered by the standards include leadership and management, teaching and learning, the classroom environment, and partnership and liaison with parents, governor(s) and other concerned parties (BDA, 2004). Examples of the standards are available on the BDA website.

The Quality Mark process is quite tightly designed. Guidance for the Quality Mark links the standards and the evidence record to the Ofsted inspection framework. As part of the process of LAs carrying out their self-audit, the guidance suggests the use of a focus group, plus representation from pupils, parents and a local dyslexia group. The progression of dyslexia-friendly qualities within an LA is indicated by auditing each standard against one of four categories of development, starting with 'focusing', and then progressing through 'developing' and 'established' to 'enhancing'. There are minimum numbers of standards acceptable for each development category.

As a first stage, 'focusing' means more than 'working toward', although it is acknowledged that, in fact, some schools will still be progressing toward meeting dyslexia-friendly criteria within the LA. At the lowest level of an LA's dyslexia-friendly development, the baseline expectations are that children with difficulties of a dyslexic nature are having their needs met appropriately, and that all statutory requirements are met. This is indicative of the difference in the authentic dyslexia-friendly approach. For some individuals and groups, including LAs, these descriptors for the 'focusing' stage might seem to suggest destinations, but to gain the dyslexia-friendly Quality Mark, this is just the beginning.

The next stage, 'developing', takes a more proactive position, requiring that good practice is promoted and supported in the LA and its schools. The 'established' category reflects the same requirements, but requires 'comprehensive evidence'. The pinnacle of an LA's dyslexia-friendly development, that of 'enhancing', requires significant evidence that high-quality practice is being shared within the LA and its schools and, further, that this good practice has potential for sharing beyond the LA. The overall expectation is that a successful dyslexia-friendly ethos means taking the message beyond the LA. This is an approach that gains greater relevance in a climate of multiagency working. It would be good practice for all professionals who are involved in working with children who experience dyslexic-type difficulties, including professionals from separate, collaborating or merging services, to know how a child is being supported and how best to help.

Evaluating the dyslexia-friendly schools initiative

The first LA to achieve dyslexia-friendly status was Liverpool, in 2005, after a three-year programme of training in which Neil MacKay and Cliff Warwick, the originators of the process, were involved. Colette O'Brien describes the project as a considerable success, with a falling number of statements for dyslexia, and fewer expressions of dissatisfaction from families (O'Brien, 2006).

Not only does this indicate that in this LA significant service and support for dyslexia no longer need to be accessed through statements of SEN, but it also suggests that schools are managing children's considerable dyslexia needs themselves, in terms of both information and resources. These outcomes match the earlier Swansea experience.

Neil MacKay, in discussing evaluation of the BDA Quality Mark, makes the interesting observation that it seems more important to families that there is dyslexia awareness among the regular members of staff in a school than it is to have a dyslexia specialist. He describes successful LAs in which the dyslexia-friendly approach is endorsed by all the advisers rather than being the province of an adviser or team for SEN, although in a number of LAs individual specialism remains the case.

Like his Liverpool colleague, MacKay notes a happier, more confident response from children, parents and practitioners in learning situations where staff feel that they have the expertise to help children and to manage a school's dyslexia requirements. (MacKay, 2006). This last is an important point. In demystifying dyslexia and linking dyslexia-friendly practice with good practice for all learners, practitioners are empowered to manage dyslexia, up to the point where children's difficulties are so significant as to require further provision.

The dyslexia-friendly schools initiative was conducted as a pilot programme, running from 2004 to 2006 with a cohort of schools in 10 LAs. By 2007, the scheme had become fully operational with significant demand (Brian Wilson, Quality Mark Development Manager, BDA, by email). This bodes well for children experiencing dyslexia-type difficulties; however, there are some issues that remain to be resolved if the dyslexia-friendly process is to realise its full potential. The funding of resources is always an issue. With the emphasis on moving dyslexia provision into schools, there are question marks hanging over the roles and, indeed, the jobs of central support team specialists. In addition, there are considerations arising from multicultural contexts and the difficulties of children whose first language is not English.

If we are all dyslexia-friendly, do we still need specialists?

However dyslexia is identified or defined in the future, it seems likely that there will continue to be a need for specialist intervention for children experiencing particularly intractable difficulties. Mainstream practitioners who have only minimal liaison opportunities with specialist teachers may wonder what practices they undertake when they withdraw children from class for individual teaching. Often specialist teachers are working through a structured programme with their pupils.

Within the specialist's repertoire, there will be knowledge and experience of the specific programmes designed to teach pupils experiencing dyslexia. These include frequently-used programmes such as the Hickey Programme (Augur, Briggs and Combley, 2000), Alpha to Omega (Hornsby and Shear, 1999), the Bangor Dyslexia Teaching System (Miles, 1989), and specialist programmes undertaken by teachers trained by the Dyslexia Institute, the Hornsby International Dyslexia Centre (now merged with Dyslexia Action), and the Helen Arkell Dyslexia Centre. In addition, there are schemes accessible to mainstream practitioners such as the multisensory teaching system for reading (MTSR) of Johnson, Phillips and Peer (1999).

The programmes usually share the common characteristics of being multisensory. They are generally strictly structured with information in small chunks, and using repetition, linking new learning with what has gone before and using overlearning to establish concepts and rules. Specialist teachers' input often extends beyond the teaching of a programme as they seek to establish ways for children to cope better with their class work, or their homework. They may also help children to learn subject-specific vocabularies and procedures. Some specialist teachers may be involved in writing individual education plans (IEPs) for the children they teach, and it is hoped that most will have opportunities to liaise with classroom practitioners.

It is not suggested that mainstream practitioners take over the dyslexia specialist's role wholesale. But with the widespread acceptance of dyslexia, and with the emphasis on early intervention, the approach to dyslexia teaching is changing. There will continue to be a need for specialist knowledge, but the expectation is that classroom practitioners will also see a role for themselves in carrying out strategic teaching and focused intervention to help children experiencing dyslexia.

Classroom practitioners may not always have access to the more specialised dyslexia teaching programmes described, but there are others that they can call on to aid their teaching. Marie Clay's reading recovery programmes have attracted a great deal of interest and support. Published programmes include *Beat Dyslexia* (Stone, 1998), Harry Cowling's publications: *Toe by Toe* (Cowling and Cowling, 1993), *The Word Wasp* (Cowling 2000), *The Hornet Literacy Primer* (Cowling, 2002), and many others. Some of these programmes support children who are experiencing reading difficulty, rather than being framed specifically around support for dyslexia, but their structured approaches follow similar precepts.

Dyslexia and multicultural considerations

One feature that modern primary schools must take into account more than ever is the recognition of, and provision for, a range of cultural models and ethnicities within their intake. When children's first language is not that of the country in which they live, there should be a support service involved. To guide them, mainstream practitioners rely on indications from teachers and helpers from the support service for pupils who have English as an alternative language (EAL). Support service staff will let class teachers know if they think that children might experience SEN distinct from language needs arising from unfamiliarity. However, it may be easier to identify a slower general rate of progress in children than to identify dyslexia. It is quite possible that dyslexic-type difficulties may at first be attributed to difficulties in language learning.

Kath Kelly (2002) makes the point that the kind of errors that might be common when pupils are gaining a second language may also resemble the errors of dyslexia, so there is scope for uncertainty as to their cause. Examples are confusion with the directing of writing from left to right, confusion with vowel sounds, and difficulty in discriminating among variations in speech sounds. Concerns regarding dyslexic-type difficulties may be identified, she suggests, by discussion with parents, by lack of interest in books, and by the persistence of difficulties identified as dyslexic in nature after children have become more familiar with the new language. Parents may be reluctant to question or challenge teachers, even though, as parents, they may have noticed difficulties at home that could be associated with dyslexia. Dyslexia-friendly practitioners would allow for the possibility of such situations arising and prepare themselves through discussion with teachers of EAL.

Bilingualism and multilingualism are of concern to many writers in the dyslexia field. Norah Frederickson and Tony Cline (2002) describe studies that show bilingual or multilingual children to be under-represented among children receiving provision for dyslexia. This situation could arise for a number of reasons, including difficulties with administrative or assessment processes. Huw Roberts (2001) and Gavin Reid (2003) describe how assessment procedures that have been adapted for use in another language may not have sufficient information about standards against which results can be measured – otherwise known as 'norms'. This means that for children who primarily use other languages, it would be difficult to carry out a reliable assessment, because there would not be enough background information to judge how far the results were typical or untypical of the group. This is as true for children whose first language is Welsh as it is for children speaking other languages, particularly in the area of common spelling differences that may influence a test. However, Reid and Fawcett (2004) confirm that progress has been made in recent years in developing assessment and intervention processes for children whose first language is not English.

Language and power relationships that may mask dyslexia

While there may be a number of reasons why children whose first language is other than English may not have difficulties of a dyslexic nature recognised and supported, there are further considerations that affect families more broadly. These are concerned with power relationships related to a dominant cultural model in schools, creating a climate wherein bilingual children are expected to change to fit the model. There may consequently be a deficit-based view of bilingual learners that, in taking English as the route to success, disregards the possibility of dyslexia as a cause of literacy difficulty.

Adrian Blackledge (2000) confirms the need for cultural change within schools. He sees literacy as culturally bound, with different meanings for, and within, societies. Blackledge's research found that teachers misperceived the interest and personal resources of mothers whose first language was not English, and targeted the most accessible parents, usually those with English backgrounds and language knowledge, when discussing how to help children at home. Quite possibly, this was unintentional and the teachers might have been horrified to realise that they were taking this position.

Practitioners in a dyslexia-friendly school would need to bear this in mind, and find a way to discuss dyslexia with teachers from the alternative language support service. This would help practitioners to have a shared understanding of how the language support teachers identify learning needs, and how best to proceed when English (or Welsh) is not children's first language. Practitioners may be able to access translators through LA sources, or informally through families.

Principles and practices

The suggestions in this section reflect the general theme of supporting the gaining of reading and writing skills when children experience significant literacy difficulties.

Some practical points about in-class support and withdrawal lessons

- In aiding children who experience dyslexia, there are two jobs to do – one is to maintain children's access to the curriculum, and the other is to help them to acquire the necessary skills to gain that access independently. A dyslexia-friendly school has a greater chance of managing these two tasks without their becoming mutually exclusive, since withdrawal lessons are not necessarily seen as both the answer to children's difficulties and the domain of the specialist.

- Where withdrawal lessons are felt to be necessary, in a dyslexia-friendly setting practitioners would expect to work closely with specialist dyslexia teachers, EAL teachers, and learning support assistants to devise, deliver and monitor input.

- Such practice carries a resource requirement: practitioners need time, space and communications means to achieve this.

A case study about a simple technique that aided reading skill and confidence

Case Study

Janey

When Janey came into the local primary school, it was hard to assess her literacy skills with certainty because she had a broad range of distracting activities, which were usually, but not always, good humoured. Her spelling was hard to judge, and the quantity of written work produced was small. After a while, her class teacher noticed that Janey avoided reading more than a few lines of any page. The teacher took her aside to listen to her read a text-based book with regular-size paragraphs. Janey made a good if faltering attempt, but gave up after a few lines and began to get rather cross.

To investigate, the teacher selected a reading book of about the same level of difficulty, but with only a few lines and a picture on each page. Janey began reading, and, turning the pages, read to the end of the book. Counting up the lines, the teacher showed her that she had in fact read the same amount of text as was in the earlier, rejected paragraph, and Janey, surprised, agreed that she had.

Next the teacher put a piece of paper under the line that Janey was reading, masking the rest of the text. This time Janey was surprised and pleased to realise that she had read a lot more of the paragraph. Janey and her teacher agreed that she got on a lot better when the text was masked in this way. Janey felt that this was a technique she could use in class without drawing attention to herself, since this was rather important to her.

Some suggestions for practitioners

It may help us to think about the values that schools transmit, and whether these carry any hidden messages. In particular, we need to be careful not to address communication predominantly to parents and carers who can communicate easily with us. When stock-purchasing time comes round, we can ask for dual-language publications to be sought out, and to be identified as resources that can go home with children for practice. When identifying possible dyslexia among children for whom English (or Welsh in a Welsh-speaking school) is not the first language, we can ask for opportunities to be made available so that we can talk in detail with the specialist teacher from the support service for alterative languages. When the specialist has concerns about children for whom English or Welsh is not their first language, we must take care to fit them into the School Action/School Action Plus model, and into the three-waves model for literacy input.

Some suggestions for parents and carers

We can ask if the LA has a dyslexia-friendly policy, and, if so, what the LA understands this to mean. We can also ask about the services available for children whose English is not their first language, and we can expect LAs to take account of cultural and linguistic differences. We can address queries of this kind to the elected member of the Council with responsibility for education, or to the officers and advisers in the LA inclusion team, or to the Director of Education or Children's Services. LAs have a deadline within which they must respond to written queries, in order to demonstrate good service.

You, as an advanced reader, can try timing yourself to see how long it takes to complete the following exercise, reflecting on what it feels like as a task, and what would make it better. Computer programs for making cloze procedures are commercially available.

You can try

A technique for easing the reading and writing load while still maintaining content: cloze procedures

Cloze procedures

Cloze procedures, or missing word _____, were developed in the 1950s _____ 1960s, and have been used in the _____ to measure reading skills. However, cloze _____ has a more interesting educational _____, allowing children experiencing dyslexic-type _____ to demonstrate their knowledge _____ having to do large amounts of writing. A cloze procedure, plus diagram or _____, can show whether a child has _____ a concept. The exercises can be _____ in many ways, bearing in _____ the need to extend the _____ of what learners are _____ to, without alarming or _____ them. Cloze procedures can be varied in the _____ and frequency of missing words. You can _____ words at regular intervals, for _____ omitting every fifth, seventh or tenth _____, or you can focus on _____ words. You can put the words in a word _____ at the bottom of the _____; these could be in order, or _____ up, or to be really challenging they could be _____, providing a chance to differentiate the _____ exercise for a class of _____ who have a wide range of _____. You can use synonyms for the _____ words. To make the task _____, you can use fewer missing _____, show the omissions not with a _____ but with a number of dashes corresponding _____ the number of letters in the missing word, and _____ put the first and/or last letter of the missing word at the _____ of the space. The _____ of the passage can of course be varied too.

Word bank (mixed): you can cross the words off as you use them

understood picture and procedure tasks varied confusing example difficulties mind without boundaries miss potential number used past word page omitted children key mixed missing words bank same line skills length to easier start even

Key points to remember

1. The dyslexia-friendly initiative is properly an authority-wide, top-down approach. Not only the province of schools or practitioners, it also represents nested policies with impact for LA, schools and classroom management.

2. The dyslexia-friendly approach is about attitude change and acceptance of the role of managing dyslexia within the school rather than about technique; teachers already have many of the strategies they need to help children experiencing dyslexia.

3. It is important not to confuse a specific learning difficulty such as dyslexia with an alternative language difficulty. Specialist teachers for English (or Welsh) as an alternative language can help here.

Further reading

Reid, G., 2005, *Dyslexia and Inclusion*, London, David Fulton Publishers

Some useful websites giving the perspective of other areas of the UK and Eire (there are other websites in addition to these)

- Eire: the Dyslexia Association of Ireland can be contacted at: www.dyslexia.ie/

- Northern Ireland: the Dyslexia Association of Northern Ireland contact is: www.nida.org.uk

- Dyslexia Scotland can be contacted at: http://dyslexiascotland.org.uk

- Dyslexia Wales can be contacted at: www.dyslexiawales.com

4

The Family View

This chapter covers some of the issues and implications for families when children experience dyslexia. It tells you about:

- views and processes in the expression of parents' and carers' concerns

- the impact of dyslexia upon family dynamics

- differences between parents' and professionals' perceptions of dyslexia

- considerations about labelling

- the value and practice of partnership working

- practical suggestions relating to developing communication with the parents and carers of children who experience dyslexia.

The difficulties surrounding dyslexia do not just affect individual children; they also affect children's families in a number of ways. Families are part of the social learning environment and are bound up with the empowerment of children experiencing a disability. There can be involvement for parents, grandparents and siblings, sometimes combining in a complex dynamic.

Children with learning characteristics that include dyslexic-type difficulties must function in a world where the demand for literacy skills is unrelenting, at least until school-leaving age and quite possibly beyond. Patrick Werquin (2006) makes the point that in an increasingly technological age, matters that would once have been dealt with orally, by speaking on the telephone or by person-to-person meetings, are now dealt with through email or telephone text messaging. The demand for literacy in a technological world is higher than ever before. The pressures upon learners to become literate, and upon their families to help them do this, are consequently greater than before.

The expression of parents' concerns

Parents generally are very conscious of the implications of literacy for the world of employment, and their concerns may be expressed when children are very young. Parents' anxieties about their children's literacy skills may lead them to approach the school, or they may choose to consult a medical practitioner. In talking to parents, it is not unusual to hear someone say, 'We knew early on that something was wrong.' What comes next is often a struggle to gain school commitment and resources. Parents, usually mothers, may follow a path of increasingly escalating strategies, beginning with trying to engage the school in discussion, but then moving on to bypassing school and the LA, mobilising private provision, or appealing to the SEN and Disability Tribunal (Griffiths, et al., 2004).

Parents and carers do not raise concerns lightly. It may take a long period of listening, talking, researching the Internet, and looking at popular magazines, television programmes and other non-academic sources, described by Griffiths et al. (2004) as 'common sense, or lay knowledge' before people ask whether their child's difficulties are dyslexic in nature. By the time the possibility of dyslexia is voiced, worried parents may have considered this so thoroughly, including reviewing their own family history, that their identification may well be correct long before a psychologist has confirmed it.

Parents' concerns should not be overlooked or dismissed, but professionals' and parents' priorities may differ. It may seem to parents that a school is ignoring their child's difficulties, whereas, in fact, the professionals are considering that child's needs in relation to the difficulties of other children, and are placing resources with those children that they consider to be most in need of them. This situation is difficult to resolve and may be complicated by the belief that resources go to those who 'shout loudest', in other words, the belief that parents who make themselves most visible, use the system, and will not take 'no' for an answer are likeliest to get results. This can lead parents to push harder, but can also lead professionals to resist harder. Added to this may be a mother's dread of being labelled a 'fussy mum' and her concerns being dismissed accordingly, or of her child being viewed in a negative way because she is raising concerns and challenging the school.

It should not be overlooked that parents have rights in this matter. Every child has the right to have his or her SEN met, and parents have the right through the 1998 Human Rights legislation to be reassured that the education received by their child is appropriate and in line with their philosophical views. It should be remembered, however, that the legislation includes a UK caveat, or exception, which states that the right to parental preference may be denied if the desired education is not compatible with the efficient provision of education, and incurs 'unreasonable public expenditure' (Schedule 3, part II, the UK Reservation to Article 2 of the First Protocol). This is the crux of many tribunal arguments, and many disability tribunal cases have been concerned in one way or another with dyslexia.

The family dynamic

The difficulties that children experience at school have implications for their home lives in a number of ways. There can be fatigue, frustration, and unhappiness when children have had difficult days. There is the question of homework, nowadays given to primary age children as a matter of course. Children who have struggled with literacy tasks during the day may well be asked to finish these as a homework task or to do some practice in what is perceived to be an area of weakness. Children with literacy-based homework will have the same difficulties of fatigue and frustration that they have experienced in their daily school work, but must face them at the end of what may have been a long and difficult day. Consequently, the homework submitted may be short in length, messy, badly spelled, or lost altogether. It may earn disapproval, disappoint practitioners, or even lead to punishment.

Parents and carers often provide homework support, but sometimes it is difficult for them to help their child. Parents too may experience dyslexia, with its accompanying difficulties and fatigue. Even without dyslexia of their own to consider, helping with homework may not be easy for parents. Their children might not want to cooperate as they are faced again with difficult, literacy-based tasks, just as they have been all day. Barbara Riddick's research confirmed that most parents find it hard to persuade their children to do additional literacy homework (Riddick, 1996). When children are willing to work at home, parents may describe long, arduous evenings of patiently helping a child to spell out or look up words, or to word-process or recopy work until there is a presentable draft to take to school.

A further factor that affects family dynamics, but that may be overlooked, is that of additional expense. There will be the cost of basic resources as children seek to carry out their school work at home. But in addition to this, and in spite of identified links between SEN and poverty or disadvantage (Reid Lyon et al., 2004), many parents will try their hardest to provide resources to help children overcome the difficulty of dyslexia. These will range from buying specialised books, spellcheckers, computers or word processors, to paying for expensive private assessments and individual lessons over a number of years. Some parents will go further, seeking a placement in a specialist school for their child. They may enter into disputes with the LA, seeking funding to support such a place or, if they can afford it, they may pay the fees themselves.

Rosemary Scott (2003) acknowledges the very difficult and complex combinations of feelings that may arise among family members, from parents determined to get the support for their children that they never had for themselves, to those who resent it once it is in place, reflecting on their own bitter school experience. Angela Fawcett describes meeting 'strong-minded women who had fought for their sons' (Fawcett, 2001: 269), while Scott also mentions that some parents can be overprotective. These experiences may give rise to situations that must be coped with by parents and children on a day-to-day basis. Grandparents may have their own experience to cope with, if they have endured school failure themselves at a time when dyslexia was not identified.

Unless a child experiencing dyslexia happens to be an only child, there is also the matter of relationships with school-age siblings. Children may be taunted by siblings as well as by peers, but the designation of dyslexia may help in such cases, providing identification and a reason for difficulty. Some of the distress that children with dyslexic-type difficulties can feel may be caused by younger siblings overtaking them in the gaining of literacy skills.

However, it should also be recognised that relationships can be positive and valuable, and should be seen in the context of a wider understanding about siblings (Connors and Stalker, 2003). While they may fight and argue, siblings may also support and defend each other in ways that are specifically relevant to their identity as members of the same family. The experience of dyslexia therefore provides only one element, of varying importance, in the family dynamic. It need not always be a negative experience.

Perceptions of dyslexia

Some difficulties are caused by a mismatch in perceptions of dyslexia between parents and professionals, ideas which themselves are subject to change and influence. Ruth Paradice's (2001) research shows that parents are strongly concerned about the emotional issues that can be present when children experience dyslexia. Professionals, however, do not attach as much importance to emotional issues, although they are aware of them. There are others aspects of dyslexia understanding in which the views of parents and professionals differ, but there is scope for a fundamental rift in the major discrepancy that Ruth Paradice describes. These contrasting points of view can contribute to the dissatisfaction some parents may experience in seeking recognition for their child's learning needs.

Angela Fawcett, who writes movingly about the difficulties she and her son Matthew faced in seeking to understand and provide for his experience of dyslexia (Fawcett, 2001, 2002), confirms the importance for parents of recognition of their child's needs. Difficulties in reaching agreement about a child's needs and how they may best be met are compounded if, as Ruth Paradice suggests, parents and professionals are not talking the same 'language'.

Issues about policy

When it comes to dyslexia, there are many areas where relationships between schools and parents can deteriorate. These include difficulties arising from differences of perception and understanding of such factors as:

- the way decisions are made regarding the allocation of resources for SEN within a school

- the assessment procedures involved

- the procedures that schools carry out to identify which children to refer to an outside agency (usually either an educational psychologist or a central support team specialist)

- the assessment procedures carried out by educational psychologists themselves

- the LA policy for the distribution of resources

- the LA policy for the management of a particular difficulty; in this case, dyslexia

- the criteria by which the LA identifies who shall have additional resources

- the implications for all these aspects of whether or not LA funding for SEN is delegated, meaning that it is passed directly to a school. This has the effect that some services may still be held and financed centrally within the LA, while others might not.

Parents, however, understandably just want their children to receive the help they need to make progress, and to be reasonably happy at school. Such aspects of SEN management and procedure may represent bureaucratic tangles which hold little relevance for parents, but which must be navigated in the bid for additional resources for their children. This can cause anger and frustration.

Further, an LA may follow a policy of not identifying dyslexia or a specific learning difficulty by name, preferring to focus on ways to meet children's learning needs. However, this view may be seen by others as a refusal to admit the existence of dyslexia, in order to avoid having to provide resources for it. This perception may give rise to dissatisfaction or hostility.

Issues about labelling

In addition to administrative and communication issues about identification, there are further issues concerned with whether or not a child should be 'labelled'. Labelling and identifying children on the grounds of difference is not a trait that all would support, since this practice can be seen as relating to a child-deficit model, concerned with a view of 'what is wrong' with the child. The SEN codes of practice signal a move away from this position when they state:

> Schools should not assume that pupils' learning difficulties always result solely, or even mainly, from problems within the young person. (DfES, 2001; National Assembly for Wales, 2002: Chapter 6, para 6:18, both codes)

However, for worried parents, labelling their child's difficulty may be a relief and a watershed, leading to an understanding of how to help the child, and to support by other parents and professionals. Further, the provision of additional services may depend upon a label being in place.

Failure to label can fuel suspicion. It is possible to hear that an LA 'won't allow' dyslexia to be identified by name, and this has been interpreted as a wish to avoid meeting responsibilities and providing resources to meet a child's learning needs. In actuality, it may be based on a valid philosophy, that it matters less that a label is given to children, than that their needs are correctly understood and appropriately met. There may even be an underlying ethical belief that it is wrong to label people. However, without an identifying label, both professionals and parents may feel either that information is being withheld, or that a child's needs are not properly understood. Once the label is in place, children, parents and practitioners may seek to find out more about the associated learning characteristics, involving themselves in understanding and meeting learning needs. For some people, therefore, the label is empowering.

In addition, there may be litigation ahead for an LA that does not provide a clear label, as it may then be argued that a child's needs have not been properly identified. Finally, labelling may depend on the specialist carrying out the assessment or diagnosis. If an educational psychologist or a paediatrician does not use a term such as 'dyslexia', professionals with less status and power are likely to feel that they must not use it either, as this would mean overriding the specialist. In such cases, the term may be avoided, yet hang in the air, making for an uncomfortable situation and leaving a parent or professional puzzled and frustrated, wondering what is at the bottom of their child's difficulty and why they cannot get a straight answer.

For some parents, encounters with professionals have given rise to strong and angry feelings that lingered in some cases for years (Murphy, 1992). Given the present support for parental views, it would be good to think that this was no longer the case, but the experience of independent support groups such as the Independent Panel for Special Education Advice (IPSEA), described in their evidence to the Parliamentary Select Committee Report Special Educational Needs (House of Commons Education and Skills Committee, 2006), suggests that unhappy experiences still occur.

Parent representation and advocacy services

The importance of parents' involvement is reinforced through the revised SEN code of practice (DfES, 2001) and the SEN code of practice for Wales (2002). Although the original code (DfE, 1994) acknowledged parents' concerns, the newer codes reflected the fact that the involvement of parents has gained a much higher profile. They focus on the need to work together with parents, and on the need to provide resolution for disagreements; this is a statutory requirement under the 1996 Education Act.

Understanding of the need to take parents and children's views into account in the meeting of children's learning needs is now a standard feature of good practice. Among the arrangements for statutory assessment of children's learning needs, the SEN codes of practice also require LAs to let parents know that they can be accompanied to meetings by friends, relatives or members of the Parent Partnership Service (Chapter 8, both codes). This kind of support or advocacy can be valuable in any joint meetings where families need to discuss their children's learning needs, not only those meetings concerned with statutory assessment.

The Parent Partnership Service provides a free source of information and help for parents who feel that they need support in talking to schools about their children. This may be viewed with scepticism by people who feel that a service that is funded by the LA cannot be neutral, and in some authorities this service, particularly in the form of disagreement resolution and mediation services, is supplied by independent providers.

Parent Partnership practitioners work hard to have a thorough knowledge of the SEN framework and to support parents, through to representation at the SEN and Disability tribunal if necessary. Parent Partnership information should be readily available through publicity in schools, Council offices and publications, and directories. For parents who do not want to use an authority's service, there are experienced independent providers available such as the Independent Panel for Special Educational Advice (IPSEA).

The Quality Mark standards: interactions with families

Aiming to improve relationships between parents and carers and schools, or authorities, Standard Four of the BDA Quality Mark process focuses upon opportunities for interaction and working together. These should include partnerships with parents, carers, children, school governors and other relevant and interested parties, but with a focus upon parents (BDA, 2004).

The standard expresses the dyslexia-friendly approach to working with parents and carers through improved communication and the availability of information. It includes the requirement to provide information about complaint processes and support groups, and about whom to talk with regarding concerns. It also includes the expectation that schools and parents should work together in the interests of children's learning.

In working with pupils, the standard raises awareness and promotes a positive educational culture that also includes children's active involvement in planning and carrying out their own learning. The focus here is upon children who have been clearly identified as experiencing dyslexia, but the expectations within the standards apply equally to children whose learning needs have not received a formal identification.

Principles and practices

The suggestions in this section reflect a general theme of developing communications with the parents and carers of children who experience dyslexia.

Some practical points about communicating school reporting processes

- When a school reporting process takes place, such as at an open evening or in the process of making evaluations for a record of achievement, there is a job of explanation to do with children. They often see a contrast between the positive comments made by a teacher, particularly to parents and carers, and the negative responses to their work that they may receive themselves.

- Responses may not be intended as negative by practitioners, or may be given greater negative weight by children because of lack of confidence. Children who experience dyslexia may sense negativity if they are unable to produce the quality of work intended. However, sometimes negative responses are voiced, perhaps because they represent the practitioner's greatest concerns, while more positive aspects remain unsaid.

- If practitioners then give too upbeat a report, emphasising positive aspects, this perceived contrast may be interpreted by children as practitioners' hypocrisy. This may also, then, become the family view.

A case study that shows the gap that might appear between parents' and schools' perceptions of a dyslexia-friendly policy

Case Study

Sean

Sean's mother had worried about his difficulties in learning to read, write and spell for some time. When she raised the question of her son's possible dyslexia with his school, she was given to understand that Sean could not have any additional help 'because it was a dyslexia-friendly school'. Sean's mother received what she felt to be appropriate attention to her son's needs only when an individual deputy head teacher took an interest. This led to the by now traditional referral for statutory assessment, leading in turn to a statement of SEN, proving that Sean's learning needs were significant and that his mother's concerns were justified. By then, Sean was approaching secondary school age, and his mother felt that too little was done too late, and that the support he received was insufficient.

It is the principle and intention of the dyslexia-friendly initiative to make situations like this a thing of the past. However, it is significant that Sean's mother came to interpret dyslexia-friendliness as a lack of help for her son, not as a provision of help.

A suggestion for practitioners: preparation for communication

We can rehearse, or at least prepare for, communication with parents and carers. What would we say to parents who disclose that they are worried about their child's reading and are wondering about dyslexia? What would we say to parents who think that their child is unhappy or is being bullied because of inability to read, write or spell very well? What about parents who say that their child cannot sleep at night, because of worry about the English SATs? How would we answer these questions if the parents' first language is not the same as our own? What would we want to know and how would we like that discussion to take place if it was about our own child? At times like these, we might find it helpful to remember the emotional impact of learning difficulties upon families, and bear in mind the sensitivities surrounding dyslexia.

A suggestion for parents and carers

If approaching a school with a view to enrolling our child, we should expect to be asked what we can say about our child's learning. If we are not asked, we can say something like, 'Would you like me to tell you how I see my child's learning needs?' This may feel a little contrived and awkward, but practitioners are likely to welcome the information.

We can have friends, relatives or advocates present when meeting to talk about our children's learning needs. It may help to have a list of points to be covered. There is no need for us to worry about producing such a list and checking it off. Education staff will appreciate the discussion being focused for them. We might also find it helpful to ask for timescales whenever any procedures, actions or referrals are discussed. While the statutory referral processes are bound by timescales, other processes are not, so timescales may not automatically be put in place.

You can try

A technique to help to build reading skills at home: paired reading

Paired reading

Paired reading is one of the techniques identified by Professor Greg Brooks (2002) as having a good impact in helping children learn to read. It is a user-friendly activity that, when carried out at home, calls on natural relationships between children who are learning to read and their families or carers.

A quiet, comfortable setting without distractions is preferable. Children choose books that they can manage or that are of interest to them, and the chosen book is discussed informally with the helper. One of the key points about paired reading is not to take the sort of approach that is formal and correcting. There is no breaking up or sounding out of words, scolding at mistakes, or allowing the child to struggle. A few minutes of paired reading every day is preferable to a large input now and again. Praise is given for success, throughout the process.

Reader and helper read the text together simultaneously, at the children's own pace. Pointing at the word can be useful – it is a matter of preference. When children come to a word they do not know, they are given a few seconds to think about it and then, if the word is not recognised, the helper can quietly and simply tell the reader what it is. It is helpful if a child then repeats the word once or twice to reinforce it.

A child may want to read alone, and a signal can be agreed as to when the helper should become silent. The helper can join in again if a child is having too much difficulty reading independently, until signalled again. Nicola Morgan at the Child Literacy Centre makes the point that 'Paired reading is about building confidence and fluency, rather than anything else'. More information about paired reading can be found at the Child Literacy Centre web page (http://childliteracy.com/) or at the Teaching Reading Writing Resources web page (www. Dundee.ac.uk/fedsoc/research/projects/).

Key points to remember

1. The emotional ramifications of dyslexia may affect not only children experiencing dyslexia-type difficulties but also their families, including parents, grandparents and siblings.

2. Perceptions of dyslexia differ, and these can cause tensions between parents and professionals. Tensions can be ameliorated by a focus on helping children to make progress.

3. When children experience dyslexia, the development of good communications and partnerships between professionals and parents or carers can aid children's progress. Parents, carers and practitioners can plan ahead for discussion, and parents can have the support of friends and relatives in informal as well as formal meetings.

Further reading

Riddick, B., Wolfe, J., and Lumsdon, D., 2002, *Dyslexia, a Practical Guide for Teachers and Parents*, London, David Fulton Publishers

Some useful websites with a focus on support for families

There are numerous sites for dyslexia, including discussion forums and retail outlets, several of which are intended for parents and carers. In addition, the folowing sites may be useful:

● iamdyslexic.com is a famous website started by Barnaby Blackburn when he was verging on his teens. It contains much valuable information together with the important perspective of individual experience.

● Bright Solutions is an American site that includes a retail function. It contains a considerable amount of information about dyslexia and can be found at www.dys-add.com/
(other dyslexia retail outlets are available in the UK).

● Sometimes parents and carers with children who experience dyslexia choose to educate their children at home. A website that provides information and support for this choice is HE-Special-UK. It can be found at: www.he-special.org.uk/

The Dyslexia-Friendly Initiative and the Local Authority (LA)

This chapter looks at what the dyslexia-friendly initiative means for LAs, and considers its impact upon them. It tells you about:

● the value to LAs of taking up the dyslexia-friendly initiative and the Quality Mark process

● the funding, support, assessment and management of dyslexia by LAs

● what LAs understand by dyslexia-friendly policies

● the scope for innovation within existing structures

● practical suggestions relating to LA policies and provisions.

LAs have a public role, and their education element is closely monitored through quality procedures. These include inspection by Ofsted and Best Quality Review, carried out by the Audit Commission. Since 2002, Councils have been subject to comprehensive performance assessment, according to the 2001 government White Paper, *Strong Local Leadership*. This process assesses a council's overall ability in eight areas, including education, and assigns a score which can be interpreted in terms of league tables, and which provides a basis for measuring improvement. The process incorporates a revised Best Value Review procedure, which continues to draw on the 'Four Cs' of Best Value: Challenge, Compare, Consult, and Compete. Councils must demonstrate progress and value for money within the key areas.

The value of the dyslexia-friendly initiative to local authorities

The purpose of the Best Value Review is to challenge entrenched approaches. It is intended to make Council function and funding receptive to new thinking and new ways of providing services, including those originating in the private sector. An examination of the dyslexia-friendly initiative in the context of the Four Cs shows that it should be a useful adjunct to Best Value. It *challenges* traditional forms of support provision, and includes *consultation* with parent and dyslexia groups. The cost-effectiveness of dyslexia-friendly policy can be *compared* usefully with other forms of provision, and it *competes* effectively with these because organisation-led training can provide a dyslexia qualification that increases expertise and creditability for the Council, as well as leading to other helpful outcomes for SEN funding in the form of reduced statements and tribunal appeals.

The adoption of a dyslexia-friendly policy can therefore help Councils and LAs to demonstrate their commitment to Best Value principles and, correspondingly, to demonstrate the improvement of quality of service. Where the entire process is embraced, the dyslexia-friendly policy is expected to be present in both LA and school development plans.

It is worth asking what other benefits there may be for an LA, not just in espousing the dyslexia-friendly policy but also in undertaking the Quality Mark procedure. After all, there are considerable resources needed to support the full dyslexia-friendly process. The cost of registration, at around £500, is not itself great, but the quality standards require the training of staff, including updating training and the provision of opportunities for dissemination and monitoring. When put together with necessary resources, these could add up to a sizeable commitment of time and materials.

An LA can justify these outgoings only if something can also be retrieved financially. In their duty to use public resources wisely, elected members of the local Council are unlikely to look kindly at increasing funding to support a dyslexia-friendly policy unless the policy also demonstrates the potential to either reduce funding elsewhere, or to gain much more quality from the money spent, and preferably both. The Swansea experience shows how the LA benefited, since the dyslexia-friendly policy released funds previously locked up in statements of SEN. More broadly, it reduced costs and the time needed for the administration of business associated with tribunal appeals.

There are also positive outcomes to be gained in a number of other ways, such as by:

- demonstrating the willingness to listen to parents and carers

- increasing the support for children with dyslexia-type learning needs in ways that do not force exasperated parents to follow the statementing route

- manifesting improvements in pupil learning outcomes in relation to targets set

- having this improvement reflected in school and LA league table outcomes

- being seen to help all learners because dyslexia-friendly methods are expected to benefit children without, as well as those with, dyslexia-type learning needs.

Adopting a dyslexia-friendly policy is only the start of the process. Care must be taken that a focus on the dyslexia-friendly initiative is not seen as removing a need for any other internal processes, provisions or controls. Not all schools need to comply with the policy in order for the LA to qualify for the Quality Mark, so the adoption of a dyslexia-friendly policy by the LA might still mean that there are some schools within its boundaries that are not following the policy. Provisions and services will need to remain available for them. There is a danger that changes or reductions in provision will be LA-wide, whether or not individual schools are following the dyslexia-friendly route. A commitment to the dyslexia-friendly policy therefore requires LAs to do their best to ensure that this includes all their schools; otherwise, there will continue to be funding issues.

SEN funding and dyslexia support

The funding of SEN remains contentious. The way in which criteria and levels of need are translated into funding arrangements varies so greatly that a survey of resourcing arrangements in England (Marsh, 2002) indicated that among the 107 respondents, there were effectively as many different patterns of funding. The government's insistence on increased delegation of funding has added to the creation of variety in funding arrangements. SEN funding is a perpetual source of tension and worry, and the matter of controlling and sharing SEN funding fairly is therefore of considerable importance to LAs. Several LAs have revised their criteria and methods for funding in recent years, although variation in criteria and in funding patterns continues.

Funding of SEN at the stages of School Action and School Action Plus is usually passed directly to schools via an agreed formula, which may differ from LA to LA. Statements of SEN provide additional resources. Sometimes money for statements is provided from the LA's overall budget for schools, rather than from some additional budget, and this may not be widely recognised. Michael Farrell (2001) considers whether funding for SEN is best served through audit-based arrangements that may operate in relation to a proportion of children identified as having SEN, or through a criteria (standards)-based system, and he concludes that the latter is the fairest.

The SEN codes of practice require LAs to publish information about their policies on SEN and their SEN processes, including assessment arrangements, explaining how SEN are funded within the LA. The codes recommend the use of assessment against the level descriptors at the end of key stages of the National Curriculum, rate of performance information, and the use of standardised screening or assessment tools to identify children experiencing significant learning needs. However, there remain variations among the criteria used by different LAs. Although this is not intended to be secret knowledge, LAs do not often publish the criteria by which judgements are made about the severity of children's educational needs, and the consequent allocation of resources. Examples of criteria for children experiencing dyslexia might include:

- working at a particular National Curriculum level in reading, writing or spelling (the LA may specify some or all of these)

- these levels being related to a certain point such as the end of a key stage

- working at a significantly lower 'age', meaning reading or spelling age in contrast to chronological age

- functioning at or below a certain percentile, in relation to a norm-related test; this has often been the second percentile (the 2 per cent level), but recent revisions by some LAs have pushed this downward to use the first percentile as the threshold

- a significant discrepancy between what is expected or predicted for individual children, and what is achieved. The discrepancy is judged in relation to test results, where an unusual level of difficulty is identified, and it may be judged in a number of ways. Depending on the LA's criteria, the discrepancy may be between the percentile level of the assessed child's literacy skills in relation to any of the following:

  - the general pupil population of the same age

  - the population of pupils of the same age and overall ability level

- other cognitive skills displayed by the assessed child
- the child's performance in other curriculum areas
- the child's own reading and listening comprehension.

The way in which dyslexia is supported in the LA relates to the way in which it is assessed, and this in turn relates to the way it is understood within the LA.

Assessment of dyslexia within local authorities

There are different approaches to the assessment of dyslexia between LAs; consequently, this is an area where there are difficulties for parents and professionals. Such differences may include the type of assessments used, the level and type of involvement of educational psychologists, and the relationship with school assessments. Although educational psychologists may choose to follow a common approach to assessment within the LA, this is not mandatory, and the choice of assessment method, together with the underlying understanding of the nature of dyslexia, may not be explained satisfactorily to parents and professionals. This situation is complicated further by the variety of practice among LAs. Moving a few yards across a country boundary may bring a parent into a completely different administrative structure, with different assessment criteria for the identification of dyslexia, and different practices for the support of children experiencing dyslexia.

Assessment by teachers is more practical and likely to be easier to comprehend, involving tests that do not require a psychologist's training. In previous years, teacher assessment for dyslexia was usually the province of the dyslexia specialist teacher. With the dyslexia-friendly initiative, it is more likely that this process will take place within school, carried out by either the SENCo or another trained member of staff. Gavin Reid emphasises the importance of assessment but points out that this should not rely only upon testing, once again highlighting the importance of the learning environment.

> Specifically, assessment should consider three aspects – difficulties, discrepancies and differences, and these should relate to the classroom environment and the curriculum. (Reid, 2005a: 11)

One of the causes of confusion surrounding the topic of dyslexia and its assessment comes from the different approaches to dyslexia that have been used over the years. Frederickson and Cline (2002) describe the early use of 'exclusion criteria' in the assessment of dyslexia. This means that when all other possible explanations for unexpected reading failure are ruled out, the difficulty may then be regarded as a specific learning difficulty in the area of literacy. This identification is based on an expectation of a certain level of intelligence in a child, and consequently does not allow for a specific learning difficulty in literacy in a child identified as having lower ability levels.

As described, discrepancy criteria have been employed frequently, with cognitive ability tests, such as the Wechsler Intelligence Scale for Children (WISC) or the British Ability Scales (BAS), being used by education psychologists to perform this function. However, there have been criticisms of this process. There are felt to be underlying conceptual difficulties with tests which claim to give an intelligence quotient (IQ) score. The basic legitimacy of IQ tests is challenged by some sources. However, others believe that they remain the best way of assessing characteristics that are associated with intelligence, and provide useful information for understanding a child's learning style and difficulties.

Ayres (1996) makes the point that cognitive assessments are sometimes driven by parents. They are aware of a difference in their child's progress, and want to know more about it and to understand it. This drive is compounded by selection procedures or 'guidance' controlling access to academic programmes and resources, so it is unlikely that cognitive testing will disappear. In seeking the detailed information embodied in a cognitive assessment, particularly if the LA is reluctant to undertake statutory assessment, concerned parents may commission private assessments from recognised dyslexia organisations, or from independent psychologists. At the time of writing, such assessments cost between £100 and £500 (according to the website beingdyslexic.co.uk).

Other factors driving the desire for independent assessment may include frustration over waiting times or frustration over an educational psychologist's preference not to use norm-based tests such as the WISC or the BAS. Sometimes there may be mistrust of the LA psychologists, based on the belief that anyone who is paid by the LA cannot be independent, or that choosing not to use IQ-type tests is a tactic to avoid recognising dyslexia. In fact, the independence of LA psychologists is respected and guarded, and is protected in the codes of practice guidance:

> Local Authorities should not have blanket policies that prevent those giving advice from commenting on the amount of provision they consider a child requires.
> (DfES, 2001; National Assembly for Wales 2002: para 7:79, both codes)

Currently, there is an attempt to move away from norm-referenced tests such as the WISC and BAS, toward a more holistic, 'multi-method, multi-measure' approach (Ayres, 1996). Assessment of dyslexia and other learning needs is expected to focus on evidence of attainment and rate of progress set against expected National Curriculum levels at a child's chronological age. There is a change of perspective in the assessment of a child's learning needs, with a greater reliance upon school assessment. This matches well with the dyslexia-friendly initiative's intention to move expertise and support, including assessment practice, into schools.

The management of dyslexia by LAs

Just as the assessment methods and criteria for gauging children's SEN may vary between LAs, so, too, may the range of provision available for children experiencing dyslexia. Schools and LAs have a certain amount of freedom in how they choose to help children, provided that practice does not flout the guidelines in the SEN codes, and provided that children make necessary progress.

Some, but not all, LAs have dyslexia units, which may be autonomous or attached to mainstream schools. They may accommodate a small number of pupils, perhaps about 10 or 12, educated in the unit. The children's length of stay might be restricted to a number of terms or years, depending on the LA's arrangements. The unit may bring children in for part of the school week, with or without operating dual registration. Alternatively, children may transfer into the unit completely for the duration of the programme, and then transfer back to their regular mainstream school when the programme finishes. Some LAs have arrangements whereby all the children with similar, significant needs attend a designated school. Some LAs have their own dyslexia schools, but most dyslexia specialist schools are likely to be independent (private).

Some mainstream schools have a base or room within the school where children experiencing dyslexia and other learning needs are taught in withdrawal lessons, but it is unlikely that they will spend much of their school time there. Children experiencing significant dyslexia are more likely to have individual or group lessons on a regular timetable, perhaps once a week, and also have a few hours of additional in-class support from a learning support assistant. For many years, the individual teaching has been provided by peripatetic specialist teachers from a central support team, working on a one-to-one or small group basis. It is this traditional model that is being challenged and superseded by the dyslexia-friendly initiative.

What do LAs understand by dyslexia-friendly policy?

An electronic enquiry of LAs in 2004 revealed that among 21 respondent LAs, 15 considered that they had a dyslexia-friendly policy, and two more were in the process of setting up such a policy. Eleven were following the dyslexia-friendly guidelines from the BDA, while some LAs were unsure what these were. The representative for one LA pointed out that they would not be able to follow the BDA Quality Mark process because there was a cost involved. The number of LAs considering that they were dyslexia-friendly, but not following the BDA process, suggests that 'dyslexia-friendly' might become a generic term. Consequently, there is a risk of dilution of the original principles, practices and standards envisaged by the BDA.

LAs that had not adopted the dyslexia-friendly initiative as defined by the BDA were still keen to outline the policies and practices that they had in place to support children experiencing dyslexia. Some were in the process of reviewing their dyslexia provision, while others described the support for dyslexia available through their specialist support team, and considered that their current processes, including training of specialists, were appropriate. Altogether, it seemed that, at least among this small group, if the LAs were not taking the BDA dyslexia-friendly path, they were still aware of it. Some LAs circulated the BDA guidelines directly to their schools.

It must be remembered, however, that no matter how well constructed a policy may be, or how well potential anomalies may have been anticipated, there may be drawbacks because of interpretation. Gary Thomas and Andrew Loxley (2001) point out that policies do not operate in isolation; they may overlay and conflict with other policies, and may be viewed or implemented differently. Policies are likely to be reinterpreted by the administrators and practitioners who encounter them. One after another, individuals may have different ideas about the policy's meaning, relevance, implications and relationship to existing practice, including funding regimes. While the BDA seeks to keep this process under control with the dyslexia-friendly Quality Mark, as has been noted, some LAs claim to be dyslexia-friendly without conforming to the quality process. It will take time to show whether such a claim can be justified.

The dyslexia-friendly standards: the Local Authority

While *Achieving Dyslexia-Friendly Schools* (BDA, 1999) gives the overall dyslexia-friendly outlook and practice, the dyslexia-friendly Quality Mark expresses these in terms of firm standards. Two of the dyslexia-friendly standards are relevant to the working of the LA. These are Standard One: Leadership and Management, and Standard Four: Partnership and Liaison with Parents, Carers, Governors and other Concerned Parties (BDA, 2004). Within Standard One, there are 11 items; within Standard Four, there are six, each ranging between 'focusing' at the lower end of the range of four categories, and 'enhancing' at the top of the range. Each item within each major standard must score somewhere on this range.

Standard One requires LAs to embed dyslexia within inclusion policies and plans, with targets relevant to dyslexia in the overarching education development plan. Dyslexia specialism or training is required for the leadership of the scheme within the LA, and within the support service, and also among appropriate LA officers and caseworkers. The standard extends the scope of the dyslexia-friendly approach to include an expectation of reduction in requests to the Parent Partnership Service over dyslexia, reduction in SENDIST tribunal cases and reduction in statements of SEN within the LA. A corresponding improvement in literacy and numeracy standards is also expected, together with requirements of support for schools in their efforts to become dyslexia-friendly.

Standard Four carries the dyslexia-friendly process into relationships between LAs, schools, governors and others. Primarily, the items within this standard reflect general good practice in the way of sharing information and procedures and listening to parents. The specific dyslexia interest is upheld by the requirement for the LA to work together with the local dyslexia associations and/or parents groups, to establish and monitor dyslexia-friendly development in local schools. The standard also gives examples of ways in which this might be done.

Principles and practices

The practical suggestions in this section focus generally upon LA's policies and provisions.

Some practical points about making information more accessible and more transparent

- LAs can make their dyslexia policy available on their websites, and make this easy to find.

- LAs can make their assessment stance available on their websites and make this easy to reach also.

- LAs can make criteria for the allocation of resources explicit on their websites, or at least make it clear that there are such criteria. LAs may argue that making criteria explicit will encourage professionals and parents to make sure that criteria are met, as if they are hurdles to be overcome. However, it is likely that this already happens, with the added frustration that at present, criteria are seen as secret, insider knowledge.

A case study that suggests a creative, flexible use of the central dyslexia specialist's time, to the benefit of a pupil

Case Study

Aaron

The dyslexia specialist teacher from the central support service arrived once a week to see Aaron. The specialist was a highly skilled person. She was interested in the many and varied characteristics of dyslexia, and had a range of multisensory techniques and apparatus (much of which she had made herself) at her disposal. Unfortunately, sometimes when she arrived at school, Aaron was absent or had to be tracked down. She designed exercises and practice work for Aaron but wished she could be in the school to see them carried out consistently. She was also aware of a number of other children in the school who experienced literacy difficulties. Nevertheless, her time was allocated to Aaron and little opportunity was available for talking to or advising the teachers separately.

The SENCo wanted to make more use of the specialist teacher's visit. As a 'one-off', he negotiated with the head teacher and the class teacher to be given time to be available one week when the specialist was due. Aaron's mother was told about the plan, and she too was supportive. When the dyslexia teacher arrived, the SENCo took over Aaron's whole class, freeing the class teacher to talk with the specialist about how she might help Aaron. The dyslexia specialist was pleased and surprised at this turn of events and judged it to be time well spent. The class teacher too was pleased to have the opportunity to talk in depth with the specialist, and felt that she was now more knowledgeable about how to help Aaron and other children who might experience dyslexic-type difficulties.

A suggestion for practitioners: to explore our potential for innovation

We can be flexible, creative and innovatory in the use of our professional skills and craft knowledge to help children who experience dyslexia. Although the National Curriculum, the Primary Strategy, and the Literacy Strategy may seem prescriptive, they all have the same purpose. That purpose is to enable children to make progress; in this case, in gaining literacy skills.

There is room for innovation through the use of IEPs. A 12-week term could, for example, provide room for three sets of four-week strategies, although this requires extra administration. The key is that innovations should be in keeping with practice approved by the school. In practical terms, this means having the agreement of the SENCo. Other possible sources of support for innovation include educational psychologists and LA advisers or advisory teachers. Innovations, including their process and content, should also be agreed with parents.

It may seem, too, that the contractual obligation of statements of SEN operate against innovation, but not if the child makes progress as a result. The annual review of the statement can change the shape of provision and intervention, and if a significant change is recommended, we can call reviews more often than annually. However, if parents and school all agree, and change is represented in the Individual Education Plans, the annual review will be sufficient. There is more about IEP target setting in Chapter 7.

A suggestion for parents and carers: ask the LA for increased access to information

We can encourage LAs to provide a dedicated helpline for parents who want to find out more about SEN, including dyslexia. Schools, the Parent Partnership Service, and independent support services all fulfil something of this function, but sometimes we want to discuss what happens in school away from that setting, and want to consider our options before embarking on a course of action. Sometimes we just want to make an initial enquiry, or talk something over, such as a proposed change or innovation. It is interesting to consider whether a helpline of this type could also be made available to children.

Further, we can encourage LAs to make their SEN processes more transparent and more accessible.

You can try

A technique that helps children experiencing dyslexia, practitioners, and administrators: getting the Mind Map® habit

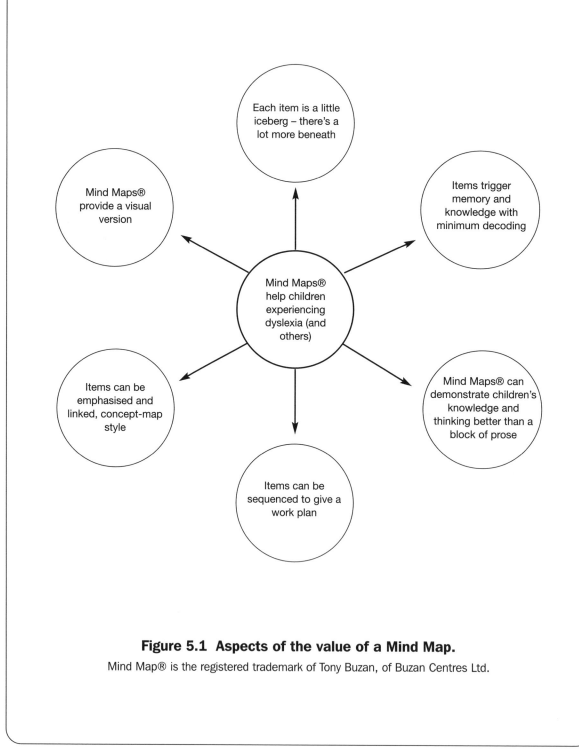

Figure 5.1 Aspects of the value of a Mind Map.

Mind Map® is the registered trademark of Tony Buzan, of Buzan Centres Ltd.

Key points to remember

1. A dyslexia-friendly policy can bring value to LAs in a number of ways, and can help with Best Value reviews.

2. There is a variety of assessment procedures and dyslexia provision that can exist within and between LAs, and information on these needs to be more readily accessible.

3. There is a need to make room for the deployment of practitioners' judgement and craft skills, and innovation, in helping children experiencing dyslexia to make progress.

Further reading

Farrell, M., 2004, *Special Educational Needs, a Resource for Practitioners*, London, Paul Chapman Publishing

Some useful websites concerning aspects of the management of dyslexia

● The BDA's main website contains many useful pages and is an authoritative source. The web address of its home page, including Quality Mark information, is: www.bdadyslexia.org.uk

● The Qualifications and Curriculum Authority publishes a list of hints for assessing for additional time in Key Stages 2 and 3, at www.qca.org.uk

● Dyslexia Action (2006) has (as the former Dyslexia Institute) published a useful booklet, *Specific Learning Difficulties*, consisting of information, addresses and resources concerned with such difficulties, including dyslexia. This is available at: www.dylsexia.org.uk/docs/SPLD_NationalResources06.pdf

6

From the Dyslexia-Friendly Local Authority (LA) to the Dyslexia-Friendly School

This chapter explores how the dyslexia-friendly initiative follows a chain of good practice from policymaking at the LA level to implementation at the school level. It tells you about:

● the measures already available in schools to help children experiencing dyslexia

● some broad characteristics to look for in order to make sure your school is dyslexia-friendly

● the experience of three practitioners in areas where dyslexia-friendly provision is being set up

● practical suggestions relating to sustaining the dyslexia-friendly approach in schools.

In considering the dyslexia-friendly initiative in the classroom, it is helpful to remember that there are already principles and policies in place to aid children experiencing dyslexia. These start with parents' right under the Human Rights Act (1998) to have the education that they want for their children, bearing in mind the UK caveat, which is also found in SEN legislation, regarding the efficient provision of education. The right of children in the UK to have their SEN met is protected by education legislation from 1981 onward. The SEN and Disability Act 2001 prevents children with disabilities from being treated differently from their non-disabled peers. It also prevents them from being refused admission to schools, and from being excluded from schools on the grounds of their disability, although there is some discussion about how this right interacts with the admission arrangements of the new academies. Access arrangements permit special considerations for children in SATs when they have been identified as having SEN, including dyslexia.

These overall principles are endorsed through the Inclusion Statement of the National Curriculum 2001. They are supported through a chain of policies that transcends change of government, the most recent of which is Removing Barriers to Achievement (DfES, 2004). National targets are set for children's reading levels at the end of Key Stages, and the National Literacy and Numeracy strategies include enhancement of the teaching of primary age children through the three-waves approach.

If this is not sufficient, the 2002 Education Act allows for the modification or disapplication of the National Curriculum for children with learning difficulties and/or disabilities, for periods of up to six months. This provision already existed for children with statements of SEN, and the 2002 Act extended it to children without such statements. All teachers are expected to be teachers of SEN, and parent representation services are (or should be) advertised in schools. Training packs and materials are available to aid the provision of support for children experiencing SEN, including children with specific learning difficulties such as dyslexia. In addition, considerable information is available through the Department for Education and Skills and other websites. The effort to improve children's literacy skills is considerable.

How dyslexia-friendly is my primary school?

Schools are not responsible for all of children's time, and external factors can interfere with learning. However, literacy failure is increasingly problematic, in a social climate that has changed considerably since the national education system was set up. Today, literacy is more important than ever in a technology- and media-led world. Competitive and aspirational social trends, combined with demographic changes, increase the importance of literacy in providing access to socially valued occupations and goods. The existence of all of the above provisions does not prevent some children from experiencing continuing literacy failure, and the dyslexia-friendly initiative urges further action in this respect.

For someone seeking reassurance that a school is dyslexia-friendly, whether practitioner, parent, or carer, there are questions to ask and things to look for, bearing in mind that LAs and schools identifying themselves as dyslexia-friendly do not always follow the requirements of the dyslexia-friendly Quality Mark.

The main question to ask is, 'What is the school's position on dyslexia?' The answer needs to be less about a focus on children's deficits and difficulties, and more about providing a good learning setting to help children experiencing dyslexia. The conversation can then move on to how this is done in the school. It would be useful if such conversations included practitioners asking parents about what they could say about their own child's learning style.

The main characteristic to look for is the use of multisensory strategies and classroom alternatives to written recording. Such strategies ideally should be seen as ordinary, rather than extraordinary. Evidence of these will include the use of technological methods as standard, both for learning and for the production of work, and a minimum of large chunks of writing to be copied from the board or from books and papers. Of course, there is much more than this to a dyslexia-friendly approach, but these ideas provide a good place to start.

The dyslexia-friendly school: the experience of three practitioners

At this stage, it is useful to turn to the real experience of practitioners working in schools that are in the process of setting up dyslexia-friendly provision. A pilot study was carried out in which three practitioners were interviewed, working in two LAs.

The first practitioner was a senior peripatetic dyslexia specialist teacher involved in setting up the dyslexia training for her LA. This LA was just in the process of realigning its provision to follow dyslexia-friendly principles. The second was a class teacher who undertook a dyslexia qualification within the training programme, in an LA where dyslexia-friendly practice was already established. The third practitioner was the head teacher of the same school. A number of issues emerged as part of the experience of these three professionals. An outline of their situations and a digest of their views are provided below.

The peripatetic teacher's experience

As a senior peripatetic dyslexia specialist, Marie (anonymised) was employed as a member of the central support service. She had been involved in setting up the training for the dyslexia-friendly initiative in the LA. Her service practitioners had focused on the primary phase, and were engaged in moving the process into the secondary phase. They had produced their own dyslexia-friendly guidelines, acknowledging the BDA input but putting it into a local context. Their LA was not following the dyslexia-friendly Quality Mark process at that time.

The dyslexia-friendly policy had resulted from a decision made at senior management level within the LA. This decision was founded partly upon the type of situation described in *Achieving Dyslexia-Friendly Schools* in which there is an escalating demand for statements on the part of schools and parents. Until the policy and provision changed, the amount of support put into schools was half an hour per week, per pupil, from the specialist teachers. Marie had certain reservations about this, because, in her experience, it did not seem to provide sufficient support, and it was expensive. She was also aware of the number of other children who would benefit from the same input but who were not given this resource; in addition, she had doubts about the efficacy of this model: 'And the children didn't learn, well, some of them do... you'll always have those few'. (Marie, dyslexia specialist teacher/trainer)

The service had devised a three-day course, paid for by the LA. This included some input from an LA psychologist, who was herself the parent of a child experiencing dyslexia. This gave her, Marie felt, an extra level of understanding. Day one of the programme covered testing, assessment, and multisensory teaching; day two covered specialised teaching programmes, whether or not they were used within that particular LA. Day three encompassed further teaching strategies. Theoretical input was kept to a minimum; the preferred focus was practical and 'hands on'. It centred upon individual examples and case studies as the teachers sought help for children they knew to have difficulties.

Attendees for the three-day course included teachers, learning support assistants, head teachers, and any other interested members of staff. One teacher from each primary school was directed by the LA to follow the course, and the training was the same for all. The programme was run twice yearly, and Marie felt that it could have been run three times a year, were it not for the constraints of funding. The costs were not in the course itself, but rather in the supply cover required to release professionals to attend. With one trained teacher so far in each primary school, the programme was advancing:

> We've got one primary school where we've so far trained, I think, five members of staff...including the Head!...I had hoped that in time we would train all the staff and we would have our first what I would consider to be truly dyslexia-friendly primary school. (Marie, dyslexia specialist teacher and trainer)

The class teacher's experience

Joanna (anonymised), a class teacher in another LA, had a different dyslexia training. She followed a module that constituted part of a master's degree course, and which would allow her to gain the Associate Member of the British Dyslexia Authority (AMBDA) qualification. An important part of this training consisted of the practical case study or studies, including teaching and assessment experience. Joanna's training was also funded by the LA, but there was a cost for the school in providing her class with a covering teacher. This, she felt, would have been the equivalent of £1,000 to £1,500 worth of cover, as the course required her to attend for nine full days throughout the year. There was an additional time requirement when Joanna was carrying out her case study, or when her assessor came to see her work.

Joanna enjoyed her training, but, as a mainstream class teacher, she found herself at a disadvantage because she was not a special needs teacher, whereas many of her fellow students were SENCos. The main difference was in their knowledge of tests and assessment protocols, and also in their specialist knowledge. She overcame this difficulty with advice from the course tutor.

Joanna was given the opportunity to give some input to fellow members of staff on an INSET (in-service training) day:

> I did probably about an hour and a half, two hours of a very brief overview of the types of activity that we do, and I thought very early on in the course...this isn't a philosophy just for children with dyslexia, this is a philosophy for the whole school...early years as well. (Joanna, class teacher)

As part of her staff development function, Joanna was also given the opportunity to work with her fellow practitioners in extending their strategies, particularly in the area of using multisensory and kinaesthetic methods, and in formulating the school development plan. This involved identifying core teaching strategies and writing them into the plan. Joanna's dyslexia training also led to the development of a role for her in carrying out assessment. Class teachers experiencing concerns about children would refer them to Joanna, and she would use the Aston Index (this is an older instrument, but still in use) and a phonological awareness test to assess their literacy learning needs.

Joanna felt that her own classroom practice had changed considerably for the better. She felt that her school could definitely be described as dyslexia-friendly, and wanted to make sure that the principles and benefits were maintained, through revising and revisiting dyslexia-friendly practices. Asked if children's SEN were now better met than in the previous years, Joanna was positive:

> I think, going by what people are saying in meetings, and teachers discussing about what they're doing in class, I would say 'yes'. I think multisensory is the way forward. I think people need to understand the rationale, and [if] you know why you're doing it in the first place, then you can be positive about it. (Joanna, class teacher)

The head teacher's experience

Colin (anonymised) was the head teacher in the school where Joanna was a class teacher. He was still in the process of getting to know his school staff, and most of his dyslexia-friendly experience came from his previous school, where he had taken the role of SENCo. Colin was in the process of bringing in ideas to improve practice, including the use of 'IEP Writer', a commercially published, computer program. He was also changing the practice of requiring children to report aloud their spelling test results, an outcome that had been drawn to his attention by concerned parents.

In line with his SENCo experience, Colin was concerned about all the pupils who came under the umbrella of experiencing SEN. Faced with the scope of the improvements he wanted to make, and the other initiatives coming into school, he did not consider himself very knowledgeable about his LA's dyslexia-friendly initiative. However, he was aware of its basic principles in terms of having a named, qualified dyslexia specialist within each school. His previous LA's dyslexia-friendly practice was among the earliest to be established: 'I think its something I've taken for granted, to be honest with you'. (Colin, head teacher)

Colin appreciated the effects of the dyslexia-friendly initiative in his school, and wanted to help children make progress through improved practice, recognising that among his staff there were matters of sensitivity as well as technique to consider. As the budget holder for the school, Colin had not been aware of the cost of cover for Joanna's training. He admitted that if she were to leave the staff, it would cause the school some financial difficulty, but that the cost would have to be borne because of the LA's dyslexia-friendly policy.

Colin was not sure how replacing Joanna's expertise would be managed; he felt that he would need to approach the local central service team for guidance about any courses and training that might be available, and would also have to look into the financial aspects. In Colin's previous school, there had not been any cover for the special needs teacher when she was out on SEN business. The school had managed within its own resources, and he described how, in his present school, he himself substituted for Joanna when she had to assess and teach children for the purpose of her case studies.

Nevertheless, replacement would be necessary. From Colin's point of view, there were considerable advantages to having trained expertise within the school, both in terms of in-service training and in terms of reassuring parents who were concerned about their children. Joanna's assessment training was particularly useful in this context, and had helped to identify learning difficulties in two children whom he felt might otherwise have gone unsupported. Colin valued the in-service training that Joanna had provided, seeing its general application for children experiencing other learning needs rather than seeing it as a matter specifically concerned with dyslexia. 'She could support us then, as class teachers, so whether we've actually gone down the road of purely dyslexia, I really don't know'. (Colin, head teacher)

Can a small/medium-size primary school be self-sufficient for dyslexia?

The practitioners interviewed above welcomed and valued the dyslexia-friendly initiative, but expressed concern about resourcing. While these individuals were mostly considering staffing resources, there is also the question of material resources if a school is to become self-sufficient in meeting the needs of children experiencing dyslexia. The ways schools are funded to meet the SEN of children may vary from LA to LA, but all will have some funding available for special needs purposes. It might be difficult for schools to commit as much funding as they would like to enable themselves to be self-sufficient in dyslexia matters, but some resources will already be in place.

Stock held by the school for use by all practitioners is likely to need larger items, such as books with high accessibility content, and computer hardware and software, as well as specific resources such as dyslexia teaching programmes with their manuals and workbooks. Library stock would need to include a wide range of age-appropriate but easy-to-read texts with both factual and fictional books, and also dual-language books.

In addition to reading and spelling tests that may be mandated by the LA, a school may need dyslexia-specific assessment materials, including phonological assessment and dyslexia-screening measures. Both of these last items are included in the CD-ROM *Learning and Teaching for Dyslexic Children*, but there are also commercially produced paper tests available, or computer-based tests such as those produced by Lucid. Schools may also benefit from having access to assessment materials and training for the use of intuitive or coloured overlays, besides keeping a stock of such overlays for children's use.

Computer programs will be needed to help children experiencing dyslexia to build necessary skills, record their work, and demonstrate their knowledge. To take advantage of these programs, children will need frequent computer access. If a child experiences motor coordination difficulty in addition to dyslexia, a larger, expanded keyboard may be a valuable aid to computer access. Laptops would be important equipment for some individual children to use in class work, and funds would need to be earmarked to meet maintenance costs for these. Other technological materials, under the general term, 'assistive software', may be necessary for access, and the recommendation of alternative ways of recording suggests the need for a variety of technological items to be available.

It soon becomes clear that acquiring such a range of resources, particularly for a small group of children, costs more that a small primary school may be able to afford. One solution is to borrow or share resources, perhaps within school clusters. Another is to have a rolling programme of building up dyslexia resources year by year. Nevertheless, it seems likely that when a child needs an exceptional, expensive resource in order to make necessary progress, schools may be forced to continue to look to the LA for additional help.

The Quality Mark standards: schools

The practitioners above described their dyslexia-friendly practice operating alongside more established forms of provision such as specialised units and withdrawal teaching. While a mixed menu of provision can be helpful because different children have different learning needs and different ways of responding, the dyslexia-friendly initiative is designed to be more than something added to existing practice; instead it seeks to produce expanding dyslexia awareness and change within an LA.

Standards Two and Four are of particular relevance to school organisation, providing guidance, including criteria and monitoring, to help schools to achieve the BDA Quality mark. Standard

Two embodies the requirement for trained staff in schools, together with access to more experienced specialist teachers. This indicates that the existence of dyslexia trained staff in schools is not intended to undermine established specialist expertise within the LA. Standard Two also provides the specifications for dyslexia training. It expects the provision of a robust training course including theory, identification, assessment, and learning programmes, together with whole-school strategies. There should be an opportunity for cascading dyslexia awareness and strategies to other school staff, and the standard suggests one working day for this purpose.

Further, the standard provides quantitative measures aimed at demonstrating children's progress, drawing on National Curriculum levels and rate of progress, as recommended by the SEN codes of practice. Qualitative measures include the development of children's self-esteem and parent confidence.

Standard Four is itself concerned with relationships with others, including parents, carers, and governors. Schools are required to let parents know early on if they are concerned about a child, and to listen, in turn, to parental concerns, with procedures in place to record any such discussions. Parents are also expected to be involved in the planning of support and intervention for their child. Altogether, it can be seen that the Quality Mark standards provide a more rigorous approach to dyslexia-friendly policy than may be evident without them.

Principles and practices

The suggestions in this section focus upon sustaining the dyslexia-friendly approach in schools.

Some practical points about staff training in schools

- Budget holders can plan ahead for dyslexia training replacement and have a contingency for that purpose.

- Dyslexia awareness and techniques can be refreshed at the start of each year. As dyslexia awareness grows, this need not and should not be left to the dyslexia-trained practitioner. Shared experience would be valuable.

- It may be difficult to engage some practitioners in dyslexia-friendly practice. A positive way forward, rather than confronting or criticising them, would be to offer opportunities for staff to discuss whether and how their practice has changed and improved, and how they would seek to move forward. Sceptics may then begin to have further thoughts, because all teachers want to help their pupils to make progress.

A case study that demonstrates a dyslexia-friendly approach to spelling tests: the revamped spelling test

Case Study

Marta

Marta was a teacher faced with the requirement of administering a weekly class spelling test. She remembered her own teacher saying, 'Hands up if you got them all wrong!', and recalled the embarrassment of the children whose hands went into the air. She remembered also that sometimes children would try to correct their mistakes in order to improve their results. If they were found out, they were roundly told off. Other children treated them as cheats and 'told' on them. In Marta's own class, there was a small group who each week spelled correctly perhaps two or three out of 10. She decided to revamp the spelling test to try to make it more dyslexia-friendly.

Marta told the children that out of 10 spellings, the first three were the ones everyone had to learn. They could learn the next three if they wanted to, and the last four if they really wanted to challenge themselves, but that there was no compulsion to do this. She decided that if children wanted to correct their spellings this was not necessarily a bad thing. It was supporting the accurate writing of the word, and she would not view it as cheating. During the week, Marta carried out a whole-class activity, breaking the three main words into their component parts, and supplementing them with little drawings as she went along. The children thought her drawings were funny, and they enjoyed the lesson, challenging Marta with their suggestions. In group work, she provided letters, modelling materials and construction materials. The children built the key words physically and could extend them or make something to remind them of the word.

There were still spelling tests once a week, but they were more relaxed, congenial affairs, and Marta did not embarrass the children by asking how many they had got wrong. She found that recording the test results as 2/3, 5/7, or 8/10, gave her more information about the children's learning than before.

A suggestion for practitioners: prompt for dyslexia-awareness training

We can signal our willingness and availability to undertake dyslexia training. We can consider whether we want this training to be part of a higher qualification, or to lead to a specialist qualification, or to be provided as in-service training (INSET), or to be part of other continuing professional development. There are several possible models of training, and these may vary from LA to LA. There may be a negative response to a query about one area of training, but a positive response to another.

In addition, as a result of our prompting, senior managers gain grounds to make enquiries about the availability of training. This availability, together with funding, could be investigated and put in place as a contingency before it becomes necessary through the exit of a trained member of staff. Encouraging the presence of a number of dyslexia-trained staff prevents a provision gap when one of them leaves.

A suggestion for parents and carers: find out about the school's dyslexia policy

We can ask whether the school has a dyslexia-friendly policy, and, if so, what the school understands this to mean in practice. Schools may say that they do not have a dyslexia-specific policy and that all children's learning needs are covered by the school's SEN policy. If we are not satisfied by this, we can ask the SEN governor or the parent governor for specific information about how children experiencing dyslexia are helped in the school. We can request also that the school look into the dyslexia-friendly initiative, allocate funds for training, and adopts its practices. To make requests of this kind gives school managers the opportunity to seek support for them from the LA.

You can try

A technique for making better use of existing resources: scrutinising photocopies for readability

Scrutinising photocopies

Modern schools rely on photocopying, especially where children with SEN, including dyslexia, are concerned. Practitioners in any primary school may make several copies per day for children for whom they want to provide something different. The cost of this resource can add up to hundreds of pounds over a year, but it is not always money well spent if the photocopies are not of good quality. Although modern photocopiers are very good, some handouts or worksheets are virtually unreadable for children who experience dyslexic-type difficulties. This is because the sheets have been overcopied and the print has become faint or is partially missing. Too much may have been crammed onto the sheet in order to save time, space and money. Sometimes the sheet has slipped in the copying and the text runs off the page. Practitioners may not notice these faults, firstly because they are good readers, and secondly because they know what the sheets are supposed to say.

Look at a photocopy as if you are someone who struggles to recognise words and letters. Are any of the above faults present? If so, then have the sheet retyped, in a bigger font (an easy-to-read font such as Ariel, preferably 14-point), split the text up into blocks of no more than five lines, and make sure there is space between areas of content. File the original as a 'master copy', and always photocopy from the 'master'.

Key points to remember

1. The three practitioners who were interviewed saw the value of dyslexia-friendly expertise to schools, and felt that pupils benefited from the dyslexia-friendly approach. They wanted it to continue and move forward.

2. Resource implications for primary schools are considerable, but scope may be found for new arrangements of sharing and pooling resources, equipment, and expertise.

3. Effort is needed to sustain the dyslexia-friendly approach through staff training and raising awareness. This includes planning ahead for when a dyslexia-trained member of staff moves on.

Further reading

MacKay, N., (2005) *Removing Dyslexia as a Barrier to Achievement*, Wakefield, SEN Marketing

Some useful websites about establishments offering dyslexia training

While many training programmes provide practitioners with the right to make decisions about special arrangements in public examinations and SATs for children who experience dyslexia, some do not. Before taking up further training, it is best to check this with the Joint Council for General Qualifications, which publishes a list of approved qualifications and corresponding programme providers.

- The BDA lists establishments that provide accredited training. These may be found at:
  www.bdadyslexia.org.uk

- Dyslexia Action has developed from the merging of the Dyslexia Institute and the Hornsby International Dyslexia Centre, combining the experience of these two important sources of dyslexia training. Its web address is:
  www.dyslexiaaction.org.uk

- The Helen Arkell Centre is the oldest established provider of dyslexia training. Its web address is:
  www.arkellcentre.org.uk

7

From the Dyslexia-Friendly School to the Dyslexia-Friendly Classroom

This chapter will help you to evaluate whether your classroom setting is dyslexia-friendly. To help you to do this, the chapter contains:

● teaching and learning considerations, including marking and individual education plan (IEP) targets

● children's views about what makes a primary school dyslexia-friendly

● assessment considerations within the classroom

● some suggestions about dyslexia-friendly resources for a limited budget

● practical suggestions and tools relating to classroom practice; these include:

– a consideration of target setting in IEPs

– a sample lesson plan with dyslexia and disability access features

– a dyslexia accessibility guide for text resources

– a self-evaluation/audit tool for developing and monitoring a dyslexia-friendly classroom.

The lesson plan, text resources guide, and self-evaluation tool are all photocopiable.

One of the changes of perspective brought about by dyslexia-friendly policy lies in the expectation that it is school practitioners, rather than external specialists, who will make the difference for a child experiencing mild to moderate dyslexic-type difficulties. If the purpose of dyslexia-friendly policy is for children to make progress, and if what happens in the classroom makes a difference, then, finally, the focus has to turn to the work of classroom practitioners in bringing about necessary change. Earlier chapters have looked at the changes in philosophical and theoretical perspectives inherent in the dyslexia-friendly initiative. Suggestions for practice change have been made throughout. The focus now is on methods of planning, monitoring and sustaining the dyslexia-friendly approach within the classroom.

Teaching and learning

For a long time, separate teaching was seen as necessary for children experiencing dyslexia. To some extent, this was because dyslexia was defined as an inability to gain skills in spite of regular teaching methods. Additionally, a career strand of dyslexia specialism developed at a time when less was known about dyslexia, and there was not the present-day emphasis upon inclusion. Children who had not been successful in learning by other methods were often found to learn from highly structured, repetitious dyslexia programmes which rehearsed and revisited small units of learning. These programmes built on what learners already knew, creating a different way of accessing literacy skills from that experienced by their peers, and were the province or specialists.

Gavin Reid (2005b) now points to a changing perspective. This indicates that what is needed for children experiencing dyslexia is adaptation and intensification of techniques already known to practitioners as part of their regular professional repertoire. While there may be common features for children with learning needs of a dyslexic nature, there are also variations, to the extent that it may no longer be necessary or useful to think of a solely specialist pedagogy.

Separately, Reid (2005a) also points out that a repetitious, isolating approach risks losing the language context and the social richness to which it is linked. While the traditional programme approach may remain valuable for children whose learning needs have proved to be particularly intractable, the overall ethos of the dyslexia-friendly initiative is that the responsibility for helping children experiencing dyslexia is increasingly that of classroom practitioners.

What do children who experience dyslexia say?

Research by Johnson and Phillips, described by Mike Johnson in 2004, was funded by the DfES and carried out in partnership with the BDA, in order to explore pupils' opinions about the kind of teaching that they felt was dyslexia-friendly. The results showed that, for pupils, good teaching was the most important characteristic of a dyslexia-friendly setting, followed jointly by the willingness of teachers to go over again what they had covered (recapitulation), and the classroom ethos that they created. The provision of resources was considerably less important to children experiencing dyslexia. Primary school children think that for dyslexia-friendly teaching, teachers should observe these guidelines:

- Check if children have understood information and instructions.
- Allow children the opportunity to ask questions.
- Avoid giving instructions too fast.
- Allow children time to think about and understand instructions.
- Allow children time to do the work.
- Ensure that children can see the board.
- Avoid rubbing out what is written on the board too soon.
- Avoid standing in front of the board.
- Avoid shouting – apart from anything else, it disrupts children's ability to think.
- Avoid embarrassing children in front of the class.

Good practice will involve listening to children's views, reflecting upon them, taking them into consideration, and acting accordingly. This last part, where action leads to change, may get overlooked for a number of reasons. For example, pupils' views may not be seen as a reason for change. Nevertheless, action leading to change is important; otherwise, the whole process of gaining pupils views is devalued.

Assessment in the class context

In the first instance, practitioners need to be able to identify children who are experiencing difficulties, and view their difficulties with some sensitivity. It serves little purpose to think of children as lazy; the likelihood is that they would prefer to please adults, and keep pace with their peers, if they could. The processes that may interfere with learning are so many and complex, that a judgement of laziness is perhaps the least useful. Sensitive practitioners use their eyes and ears to notice when and in which tasks children experience difficulties, and also to notice which approaches gain a good response. Teaching and working diagnostically in this way, sensitive practitioners can use every new piece of information and understanding that they gain about a child's learning, to contribute to their own effective practice.

Baseline assessments, reading and spelling tests, SATs and other assessment processes are already in place in the primary school, providing information about a child's literacy levels. However, observation can add quality to these and provide a key to progress. What should the practitioner be noticing? MacKay (2005: 172) suggests looking for a 'pattern of strengths and weaknesses', this would highlight the 'unexpected difficulty' described in the British Psychological Society definition. Moreover, as in the case study below, a consideration of the learning environment may show that a child's attitude to the task set, even to the extent of 'acting out' and violent behaviour, can indicate a learning difficulty.

Rather than focusing upon a child's perceived shortcomings, it would be best if the observer's attention focused on the dynamics of the setting and the social context. However, observation needs an extra adult to be available, and this is not always easy to arrange. It would be advisable, and ethical, to have a parent's or carer's agreement before undertaking observation.

Prescribed literacy requirements

All teaching can inform practitioners' understanding of how children learn, especially when children are experiencing literacy difficulties. The continued and consistent practice of hearing children read obviously tells the practitioner a great deal about their difficulties, especially if a miscue analysis is carried out, as shown below. However, in the mainstream primary school, literacy has such an important focus that it is underpinned with strongly prescribed approaches, with which all practitioners have to be familiar. The content of the National Curriculum is delivered through the process of the literacy strategy within the primary strategy, by means of the Literacy Hour. Within these carefully structured requirements, the question remains as to how practitioners can help children who do not make necessary progress in literacy, since present-day education also requires personalised learning.

Dorothy Smith (2000) makes the point that the Literacy Hour may benefit children experiencing dyslexia because it is closely organised and structured. For work at text level, shared work and plenary work, there is no reason why children with dyslexic-type difficulties should not participate and contribute in the same way as children without such difficulties. However, word-level work is where children experiencing dyslexia might need a more individualised approach, which requires further organisation on the part of practitioners.

Creative ways need to be found to make tasks relevant but also manageable for children experiencing dyslexia. They need ways of showing their knowledge, and should not be 'setted' in a low-achieving, low-ability group. A decision has to be made whether any individual intervention programme work takes place within the Literacy Hour or external to it, but Dorothy Smith points out that a certain amount of flexibility is possible within the National Literacy Strategy, and that its objectives and interventions can be matched. It is also true that literacy activities take place throughout the day, not just in the literacy hour, and care needs to be taken to make those activities similarly accessible.

Marking

In terms of classroom practice, the question of marking should also be considered. Schools should have marking policies in place that are clear and followed by the whole staff. It would be helpful if the marking policy gave guidance for marking the work of children who experience dyslexia. This could then be made clear to children themselves as well as to parents and practitioners.

There is a general feeling that covering a page with red ink corrections is not altogether helpful, since it is a depressing sight that both discourages the learner and makes it difficult to see the original work. Today, marking is often limited to a portion of the writing rather than the whole, and some markers will avoid red ink, with its connotations of failure. In spite of modern trends, both of these approaches can disturb those who feel that a page closely marked in red ink is a sign of a marker's job properly done.

Writing in a secondary context, Riddick et al. (2002) recommend marking with two pens (neither of which would be red); one for structure, and the other for content and ideas. The BDA also recommends the use of two pens; this time, one is for content, and the other for spelling and presentation, correcting only those spellings that have been taught. Either method would require marking a piece twice, or swapping pens, and both methods may be difficult practically. Nor will different colours of marking help a child whose colour vision is affected or who is reading through a coloured overlay.

Nevertheless, it is important that the purpose of marking is made clear. Too often, marking focuses on spelling and grammar; this has been the convention, and not to mark in this way may attract criticism for the teacher. For children experiencing dyslexia, this means that their work is always likely to be adversely marked. In addition, they may not be able to make out a teacher's own written comments unless the handwriting is very clear. Overall, advice seems generally to be to mark for content. Comments should be positive.

The DfES (2005) CD-ROM, *Learning and Teaching for Dyslexic Children*, gives some useful guidance. It suggests that work be marked only in relation to the learning objective, which has been explained to children beforehand, so that they understand what is being marked and why. Further, it suggests that only one or two errors be identified and that these should relate to what children have already been taught. It is best to mark with the child present, and to suggest ways of avoiding the same error in the future.

There are some other useful points to consider. Dyslexia Action suggests that if spelling is particularly weak, ticks can be placed on words that are correct rather than corrections placed on all the errors. Another helpful strategy is to tick a line where no errors are made, using a dot in the margin to indicate an error.

A further important point to make about marking has been emphasised by Neil MacKay (given in an address at the Conference of the UK Literacy Association, 2005). He points out that if in the dyslexia-friendly classroom alternative methods of recording work are going to be encouraged, marking has to take account of this. Whatever the format, similar considerations apply; it has to be clear what is being marked, whether content, ideas, accuracy, technique, or presentation.

Spending £50 to make my classroom more dyslexia-friendly

At this point, it is relevant to consider the question of resources. The cost of resourcing the dyslexia-friendly initiative within the classroom is not much addressed, so the issue is worth considering here. While a primary classroom that is properly stocked for general purposes will have many useful materials and resources, it would also be advisable to have some materials with dyslexia in mind.

For older children in the primary school, practitioners might want to have some games and resource items that support multisensory learning but that do not look immature to sensitive children. Alphabet-sequencing resources will still be useful, because these are important for dictionary and index activities. A magnetic board with magnetic words and letters would be valuable, plus extra magnetic strips to add to other shapes and outlines as required. In addition, the *ACE Spelling Dictionary* (Moseley, 1995; available from the LDA) is well thought of, so a copy of this in the classroom with a book of exercises to go with it would be helpful (available from the TTS Group, Nottinghamshire, or Amazon). Practitioners would need to take the time to read and understand the method behind the *ACE Spelling Dictionary* in order for it to be effectively employed.

A short shopping list would easily use up a £50 budget, but if there was more money available, a class selection of readers that are age-appropriate and of high interest, but with accessible text for children who find reading difficult, would be valuable. An up-to-date list of reading resources is provided by Suzanne Baker (2006).

The dyslexia-friendly standards: classrooms

Standard Three of the Dyslexia-Friendly Quality Mark Initiative (BDA, 2004) focuses on the classroom environment. Requirements for the classroom are relatively modest and are linked to the LA through the identification, monitoring and sharing of good practice. To meet the standard, LAs are expected to promote the development of self-review for the classroom, and to monitor the use of recognised dyslexia-friendly access strategies, making the classroom learner-oriented. Suggestions for a self-review process, together with other planning and self-monitoring tools, are given below.

Principles and practices

The suggestions in this section represent practical aspects of classroom work.

Some practical points about target setting in IEPs

- Make IEPs based on the learning setting, rather than on child deficit. They should say what practitioners are going to do, and how the learning setting is going to be changed, to bring about necessary progress for a child. There should always be a built-in expectation that such progress will take place, even if targets are set cautiously.

- It is generally considered advisable that children should be involved in setting targets for themselves, but care must be taken that this process does not cause children to feel inadequate in their literacy skills.

- Reading targets may be based on any number of attributes – months of gain in reading age; completion of a particular book or scheme; number of words, lines, paragraphs or pages read on a regular basis; number of times per week a child is heard reading; completion of a level in a computer program; amount of time on task; amount of autonomy; reaching a National Curriculum level within a time frame; answering questions related to the text; and so on – the possibilities are limited only by imagination.

- Other targets for a child experiencing dyslexia may relate to developing characteristics such as phonological awareness, identifying rhyme, building phonic blends, focusing on word endings, establishing correct visual direction, etc., all through designated tasks.

- The possibilities are endless but the aim, as always, is that children should make recognisable progress, and if the targets are clear, the methods should follow from them. The kind of focus that is possible for reading targets also applies to spelling and writing skills.

- Whether or not IEPs are ever replaced by an alternative method of monitoring pupil's programmes and progress, targets and programmes for an individual child should follow the SMART outline. Citing Lloyd and Berthelot (1992), Gavin Reid (2005c) gives the original configuration of these as specific, measurable, achievable, relevant and timely. Modified by popular usage, one may also hear variations such as short, manageable, achievable, reviewed and timed. All these will work. The point is that targets are not useful to children if they are broad and open-ended, carried over from one IEP review to another without change.

Some photocopiable resources to support a dyslexia-friendly approach

Three photocopiable resources are offered here to help practitioners to maintain a dyslexia-friendly perspective:

- a sample lesson plan that accommodates dyslexia and other disability access needs
- a dyslexia accessibility guide for making and monitoring text resources
- a self-evaluation/audit tool that asks: how dyslexia-friendly is my primary classroom?

These are offered as models or suggestions, and practitioners are free to amend them in order to develop their dyslexia-friendly involvement as they see fit.

A sample lesson plan

Working practitioners have their own ways of recording and planning, probably based in part on what they were taught in their training, and in part on what their head teacher requests. As a result of the literacy and numeracy strategies, the school improvement agenda, and the National Curriculum, practice is quite closely prescribed already, and this includes planning. It is not the intention to impose a further layer of lesson planning on top of those processes already in use. However, the attached lesson plan model takes account of the dyslexia-friendly approach, and, in giving space to individual access arrangements, acknowledges the duty to promote opportunity for disabled people under the Disability Discrimination Act as amended in 2005.

Practitioners can use this model to monitor their own practice by occasionally planning out a lesson in the format shown here. Lesson attributes can be checked off from the dyslexia access list, and highlighted if not present, with the intention that further lessons will cover all the elements in due course.

Text resources dyslexia accessibility guide

The checklist that forms this guide can be used to monitor established resources or to build new ones. The guide ensures that all written resources placed before children experiencing dyslexia are as accessible as possible. When practitioners have used the guide a couple of times in monitoring or producing resources, the process becomes routine. Again, it is suggested that schemes and resources are monitored at manageable intervals.

A self-evaluation/audit tool: how Dyslexia-friendly is my primary classroom?

This self-evaluation checklist and audit tool is drawn from a number of sources that include both literature and experience. Its purpose is to provide practitioners with a memory aid, to remind them about dyslexia-friendly classroom characteristics. The self-evaluation/audit tool is in two parts. The first part considers the classroom learning setting; the second part considers the classroom within the larger school setting, looking at the support needed from the school by practitioners seeking to establish a dyslexia-friendly ethos in the classroom.

Sample lesson plan for a dyslexia-friendly class

Date				Topic:
Learning Outcomes				

Time	Teacher activity	Learner activity	Supporter activity	Material resources	Dyslexia access reminders
					Visual input
					Aural input
					Kinaesthetic input
					All these close together
					Materials checked to be dyslexia-friendly
					Short spelling list
					Scaffolded writing
					Minimum board copying
					Use of diagrams, charts
					Small work chunks
					Individual targets
					Recapitulation
					Opportunities for:
					● extra time
					● working with peers
					● showing knowledge
					● pupil ICT use

Access arrangements for individual children

Assessment of outcomes

(B. Pavey, adapted from Hillier, 2002).

Text Resources Dyslexia Accessibility Guide

Readability

Reading age of text checked for accessibility ☐

Interest level of text appropriate to age range ☐

Font/print clearly distinguishable, with rounded shape (preferably 14-pt) ☐

Photocopy clean and clear ☐

Text in small groups: five lines maximum ☐

Frequent subheadings, shown in bold ☐

Off-white or tinted paper ☐

Layout

Blocks of text are clearly separated ☐

Headings/subheadings are clearly separated from text ☐

Diagrams and illustrations are used ☐

Bullet points or numbered lists are used ☐

Diagrams/illustrations give the same information as, or relate to, the text ☐

Diagrams and illustrations are near relevant text ☐

Colour is used as a visual identifier: highlighting, colour coding, blocks of colour isolating important content ☐

Instructions

Instructions are clearly identified on page ☐

Instructions are clearly broken down into small steps ☐

Statements are clear, without ambiguity (check with another person) ☐

Timescale is clearly stated ☐

Amount of work to be produced is clearly stated ☐

Assessment/marking criteria are clearly stated ☐

Content and concepts

Subject-specific words are linked to clear concepts, and are clearly explained, reinforced, and spelled ☐

A glossary/key words/ vocabulary list is provided ☐

Subject-specific techniques have written or diagrammed reminders and guidelines ☐

The self-evaluation/audit tool does not address the professional teaching of reading. It seeks to take a social model approach in moving the emphasis away from child deficit and toward the improvement of the learning setting. For this reason, it does not focus on individual learning characteristics. For anyone seeking this information, lists can be found in the literature or on the BDA website. The self-evaluation/audit tool covers the following areas:

Part One: The dyslexia-friendly classroom

A. Text resources available in the classroom

B. Focused dyslexia-friendly teaching to support literacy skills

C. Classroom arrangements

D. Affective aspects

E. Classroom interactions

F. General dyslexia-friendly teaching and learning

Part Two: The dyslexia-friendly classroom within the school setting

In scoring the self-evaluation/audit tool, responses should be anonymised, and scores for the items should certainly not be used as an identifier of any practitioner's difficulty. Nevertheless, the checklist can serve a useful purpose, because without self-monitoring it is possible to drift away from the best conditions, and because carrying out the audit is evidence of the developing self-evaluation process required by Standard Three of the Quality Mark protocol.

Practitioners can complete the checklist at agreed intervals, at least annually, and can compare it with their own results year by year, and if there are other adults attached to the class, they might compare results with each other. Alternatively, the classroom adults can complete the evaluation as a group, or by having someone else evaluate them. It could be that older children complete the evaluation. Additionally, the audit tool could be used as a whole-school self-evaluation. Items may be added. It does not matter too much how the evaluation is done, because the main purpose is to revisit dyslexia-friendly characteristics and assess classroom progress toward a good ethos. The process could be completed annually, providing a quality cycle (Fig 7.1).

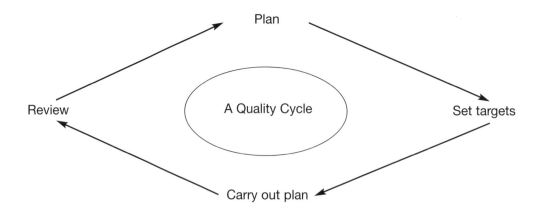

Figure 7.1 The continuous process of a quality cycle

Audit tool items are scored by ticking a box for each one, using a scale with the categories 'never', 'sometimes' (less than 50 per cent), 'middling' (about 50 per cent), 'usually' (more than

50 per cent), and 'always'. The self evaluation/audit tool is divided into seven areas, six for the classroom and one for the school, and each can be scrutinised to see which areas are the weakest and which are the strongest. The aim of the process is, of course, to increase the number of ticks in the 'usually' and 'always' boxes in Part One, and the 'I think Yes' box in Part Two, and to use low-scoring items, or areas, as a basis for future developments.

Scores should not be given too much prominence as a source of measurement. The self-evaluation tool simply brings together recommendations for good dyslexia-friendly practice, and invites practitioners to see where there are strengths and where there is scope for development. The self-evaluation/audit tool is located at the end of this chapter.

A case study that shows the value of observation in understanding a child's learning needs

Case Study

Tony

Nine-year-old Tony's mother was worried about the reports that she was getting regarding his behaviour in class. He seemed to be disruptive, and at times aggressive. He damaged resources and furniture, would not settle to his work, shouted out, and 'answered back' to the teacher. His mother knew Tony to be a bright and lively boy, interested in everything, constantly building and designing with his construction kits. She expressed her concerns to the SENCo.

The SENCo looked at Tony's reading test results. He had gained some basic reading skills, and these did not immediately given cause for concern. She then looked at his drawing and writing and was immediately struck by how different these were from the work of other children. In drawing, the marks were large, black and straight, as if gone over many times. The written work was of small amounts, untidy and frequently rubbed out. Consequently, it was difficult to make a judgement about spelling.

With his mother's agreement, the SENCo asked a learning support assistant to sit at the back of Tony's class and list what happened for one morning over three consecutive weeks. At the end of this period, the SENCo could see that Tony's behaviours were at their most problematic when there was a strong written work element, particularly in the handwriting sessions. At these times, he would sharpen his pencil; move around the room; and lose, and then seek, erasers, rulers or paper. He would regularly rub out and eventually destroy his work. He would attempt to strike up conversations with other children, sometimes hitting them. He would move the furniture about noisily, sit in awkward positions, and fall off his chair. Sometimes he would try to involve the teacher in a conversation; this could then become argumentative. Overall, it was clear to see that the written work task was causing Tony considerable difficulty, and possibly quite a lot of stress.

When the observation was discussed by the SENCo, the head teacher, the class teacher and Tony's mother, they agreed that their concerns were sufficient to ask the educational psychologist to become involved. A cognitive assessment confirmed that Tony experienced significant learning difficulty in literacy skills, particularly where writing and spelling were concerned. Although Tony had gained some reading skills, these were not in line with his evident ability in other areas. They had masked the real difficulties that he was experiencing.

A suggestion for practitioners: making opportunities for observation

We can try to ensure that there is room in our busy schedules to carry out observations such as the one described above. This may be difficult because time is allocated to helping children by working directly with them, and there is always likely to be more demand for help than there is help available to give. However, the case study shows how observation can be used to understand a child's learning needs when otherwise they may be misunderstood, masked by other characteristics. Precious time taken to observe objectively a child experiencing difficulties can result in support better focused to help them. The dyslexia-friendly focus enables observation practice such as this to move away from the province of an education psychologist to that of a school's practitioners.

A suggestion for parents and careers: let us have dyslexia-friendly input too

When a school takes the dyslexia-friendly approach, we can ask via parent representation or via the SEN governor for the school to provide dyslexia-friendly guidance for any of us who are interested. Included in this process should be accessible input for adults when English is not their first language. Guidance of this kind could lead to increased understanding of a school's approach to dyslexia and enable us to carry over the approaches in the home setting where appropriate, as well as helping to build a mutually supportive home/school process. Shaping dyslexia-friendly guidance for parents and carers would help schools to clarify their dyslexia support processes for themselves.

You can try

A technique used to gain a better understanding of how children experiencing dyslexia approach their reading tasks, and the types of errors they make, making it easier to focus appropriate teaching: carrying out a miscue analysis

Miscue analysis

Miscue analysis is a useful process that has been one of the tools of the SENCo. It is not a difficult process, and once they have learnt it, mainstream practitioners can use it to identify the kinds of errors that children are making when they are learning to read, and to design an intervention that will help to overcome them. The likelihood is that if one child experiences such errors so may another, and practitioners can build up a bank of resources to help overcome common errors.

To carry out a miscue analysis, you need a text that the individual child can read with some skill so that not all the words are error prone, but also one that is not so easy that there are no errors. You can decide whether the text has a picture or not, to enable the reader to have contextual clues. You can also let children choose the text that they read, as this informs your understanding of what kind of choices they make for themselves. It does not need to be a long text, just long enough to display a pattern of errors. It also needs to be a text that the child has not read before.

To begin the miscue analysis, you need an identical copy, usually a photocopy, of the text the child is reading. On your copy, as the child reads, you mark refusals, omissions, non-responses, substitution, hesitation, self-correction, or repetition (Reid, 2005a). Some teachers underline or cross out the affected word, and you can write in the alternatives offered by the child when reading words erroneously. Systems often show coding symbols attached to this process, but teachers could inscribe the text in ways that suit themselves, since the analysis is for their own use only (although it has been used in the past as a measurement process).

Once the text has been inscribed with the errors, quite a lot of information can be gained from this process. The errors can be counted to see if any prevail, or whether there is an even spread. Children's choices of text can be scrutinised to see whether they are similar to texts used regularly in the classroom or whether their preferred choice is something quite different. You can tell from the kind of errors how children go about attacking the reading of words. You can also tell whether children have an understanding of the text, and whether they are taking a lead from contextual clues.

Omissions and reversals may suggest a difficulty with visual tracking. Errors that are in words that resemble other words may indicate a lack of transfer of visual or aural patterns and sequences. Getting a word wrong that was previously correct may say something about memory. Self-correction suggests a strategy worth further investigation. What are readers responding to that helps them make a positive change? Word choices indicate whether contextual cues are being relied upon. Does reading improve when only one or two lines are visible? If so, masking lower lines can be used as a strategy to aid reading.

You can practise with a friend who is pretending to be a reader making errors; it takes only one go to get the hang of it. If you doubt your ability to keep up with the speed of children's reading, a reader can be taped and the miscues analysed afterward. This process will provide more information than many reading tests. It is not subject to the 'practice effect' that can result in children learning the test, and is more natural and comfortable for children.

The DfES has a considerably more detailed description of miscue analysis on its website: www.dfes.gov.uk/readwriteplus/bank/Miscue

Key points to remember

1. Although the full dyslexia-friendly initiative is a top-down process, following a lead set by the LA, there is a great deal that practitioners can do to make classroom interactions and resources more supportive of children who experience dyslexia.

2. The process of maintaining an internal dyslexia-friendly policy will be helped by a quality review cycle based upon a self-review process. This process can be carried out by practitioners as individuals or as a group.

3. Good practice requires listening to children's views, and involving parents and carers in knowledge of the dyslexia-friendly process.

Further reading

British Dyslexia Association (BDA) (2005) *Achieving Dyslexia-Friendly Schools* (5th edn) Reading, BDA, available online at:
www.bdaweb.co.uk/bda/downloads/wholedocument.pdf

Some useful websites to help primary schools to sustain their dyslexia-friendly approach

- The SNAP (special needs assessment profile) website has contributions from three highly respected professionals: Charles Weedon, Gavin Reid and Rob Long. It contains screening and assessment materials, resources and advice. It can be found at:
  www.SNAPassessment.com

- The original BDA publication, *Achieving Dyslexia-Friendly Schools* can be downloaded free. It can be found at:
  www.bdaweb.co.uk/bda/downloads/wholedocument.pdf

- Schools can obtain a copy of the free CD-ROM from the DfES, *Learning and Teaching for Dyslexic Children* (ref. DfES, 1184-2005), and the content is downloadable from www.standards.dfes.gov.uk following this path:

Standards Site home; Primary National Strategy; Publications; Inclusion; Teaching and Learning for Dyslexic Children. The CD-ROM itself is available from the DfES Publications Centre.

Date: ....

Self Evaluation/Audit Tool: How dyslexia-friendly is my primary classroom?
Part 1: The dyslexia-friendly classroom

A. Text resources available in the classroom	Never	Sometimes (less than 50%)	Middling (about 50%)	Usually (more than 50%)	Always
1. Reading age of text is checked for accessibility					
2. Interest level of text is appropriate to age range					
3. Font is clearly distinguishable, with rounded shape, preferably in size 14-pt					
4. Photocopies are clean and clear					
5. Text is in small groups: five lines maximum					
6. There are frequent subheadings, shown in bold					
7. Off-white or tinted paper is used					
8. Blocks of text are clearly separated					
9. Headings/subheadings are clearly separated from text					
10. Diagrams and illustrations are used					
11. Diagrams and illustrations give same information, or relate to, text					
12. Diagrams and illustrations are near relevant text					
Total					

B. Focused dyslexia-friendly teaching to support literacy skills	Never	Sometimes (less than 50%)	Middling (about 50%)	Usually (more than 50%)	Always
1. Spelling tests are short and differentiated					
2. Rhyming skills are taught visually and aurally					
3. Mnemonics are used to help children remember spellings					
4. Cloze procedures are used to vary writing tasks					
5. Writing frames are used to support writing tasks					
6. Miscue analysis is used to gain understanding of children's reading difficulties					
7. Texts are broken down into small chunks					
8. Instructions are broken down into small parts					
9. Sequencing is taught as a skill					
10. SMART targets are used in IEPs					
11. 'Concrete' literacy targets are used in IEPs					
12. Texts are given to children ahead of time for practice purposes					
Total					

C. Classroom arrangements	Never	Sometimes (less than 50%)	Middling (about 50%)	Usually (more than 50%)	Always
1. Care is taken so that children with possible dyslexia see and hear teacher clearly					
2. Children experiencing possible dyslexia have opportunities to work with their peers					
3. Children experiencing possible dyslexia have opportunities to work in a quiet area					
4. Children experiencing possible dyslexia have opportunities to display their understanding					
5. Items in classrooms are clearly labelled					
6. Labels include languages other than English where children have different languages					
7. Practitioners' handwriting is clear					
8. Avoided: rapid change in classroom layout					
9. Visual displays conform to text resource guidelines (see section A above)					
10. Children experiencing possible dyslexia can use a computer to produce class work					
11. Children experiencing possible dyslexia can use a computer to produce homework					
12. Relevant literacy apparatus is available for children to use if they feel the need					
13. Coloured overlays are available if children are assessed as benefiting from them					
14. Children who request tinted paper may have it					
15. Practical apparatus is available regardless of age					
Total					

D. Affective aspects	Never	Sometimes (less than 50%)	Middling (about 50%)	Usually (more than 50%)	Always
1. Practitioners know and use children's preferred individual learning styles (particularly visual, auditory or kinaesthetic)					
2. Practitioners challenge children to use different learning styles, in a manageable way					
3. Practitioners know their own preferred individual learning styles (their comfort zone)					
4. Practitioners challenge themselves to move outside their own comfort zone					
5. Avoided: judgements of laziness					
6. Avoided: the giving of punishment for small amounts of work					
7. Children are praised and reassured even for a small amount of work					
8. Children's reading in front of class is voluntary (rather than by adult selection)					
9. Children's writing on the board or in front of class is voluntary					
10. Children's spelling aloud or on the board is voluntary					
11. There is a reward system in class					
12. Rewards can be achieved by all the children in the class					
13. Learning tasks consider and deal with emotional issues first					
14. Care is taken that children are not teased for literacy difficulties					
15. Care is taken that extra work time does not eliminate enjoyed activities (break, golden time)					
16. Care is taken to protect children's feelings					
Total					

E. Classroom interactions	Never	Sometimes (less than 50%)	Middling (about 50%)	Usually (more than 50%)	Always
1. Practitioners' concerns about children's literacy are respected					
2. Parents' and carers' concerns about their children's literacy are respected					
3. Children's concerns about their own literacy are respected					
4. Avoided: use of loud, raised voice by practitioner (it destroys thinking)					
5. Home/school diaries include praise					
6. Classroom practitioners meet with English as alternative language specialist(s)					
7. Classroom practitioners meet with dyslexia specialist(s)					
8. Classroom practitioners meet with speech and language specialist(s)					
9. There are opportunities to observe classroom interactions when a child experiences literacy difficulties					
10. Avoided: ranking of children according to their literacy skills					
11. Attendance of children experiencing possible or actual dyslexia is high					
Total					

F. General dyslexia-friendly teaching and learning	Never	Sometimes (less than 50%)	Middling (about 50%)	Usually (more than 50%)	Always
Teaching					
1. Instructions are clearly identified on the page or board					
2. Statements are clear, without ambiguity (check with another person)					
3. Explanations are repeated, in different ways, as children require					
4. Timescale of a task is clearly stated, supportively (see no.5 below)					
5. Extra time is allowed for children to finish written work if necessary					
6. Length of product (how much the children are expected to do) is clearly stated					
7. Length of product makes allowances for dyslexia					
8. Subject specific words are linked to clear concepts					
9. Practitioner talking is reduced (maximum 10 mins.)					
10. Board copying is reduced (maximum five lines)					
11. Handouts are available to reduce board copying (following guidelines in section A)					
12. Input is given in small 'chunks'					
13. Input takes account of multisensory learning – visual, auditory, kinaesthetic					
14. VAK stimuli and tasks are close together					
15. Teaching uses diagrams and illustrations					
16. Teaching uses bullet points and lists					
17. Colour is used as an identifier: colour coding, highlighting, and colour blocks for focus					
18. New concepts are linked to previous concepts					
19. New techniques are linked to previous techniques					
20. Changes acknowledge what children say about how best they learn					

F. General dyslexia-friendly teaching and learning	Never	Sometimes (less than 50%)	Middling (about 50%)	Usually (more than 50%)	Always
21. Assessment/marking criteria are clearly stated, including those for alternative formats					
Learning					
22. Children's output uses diagrams and illustrations					
23. Children's output uses bullet points and numbered lists					
24. Children can use alternative means of recording; e.g., poster, tape, ICT					
25. Children are allowed (or encouraged) to do the picture first					
26. Children are asked how best they learn					
27. Children are allowed to ask questions					
28. Children's output is judged on quality and content					
Total					

Evaluation/Audit Tool: How dyslexia-friendly is my classroom?
Part 2: The dyslexia-friendly classroom within the school setting

	I Think No	Unsure	I Think Yes
1. There is a school marking policy in use.			
2. There is a school reading policy in use.			
3. There is a school handwriting policy in use.			
4. There is a school spelling policy in use.			
5. There is a shared understanding of the point at which concerns about a child's reading, spelling or handwriting are discussed with parents or carers.			
6. There is a shared understanding about the point at which concerns about a child's reading, spelling or handwriting are discussed with the SENCo.			
7. There is a shared understanding about the point at which dyslexia-specific assessments are carried out in school for a child.			
8. There is a shared understanding about the point at which advice external to the school should be sought when it is suspected that a child may experience dyslexia.			
9. There are dyslexia-assessment materials for use within school.			
10. There is access to at least one dyslexia-specific programme within the school for use in helping children who experience dyslexia.			
11. There are dyslexia-friendly books in the school library with age-appropriate interest but with text that is of a reduced amount and accessible for children who find reading difficult.			
12. Dyslexia-friendly books are easy for readers to find.			
13. Dyslexia-friendly books are indicated in a way that is not embarrassing for children.			
14. The presence of dyslexia-friendly books in the library is checked by eye, not just by catalogue.			
15. There are dyslexia-support ICT programmes within the school.			
Total			

To conclude the self-evaluation process

1. Which do you think are the most important out of all the self-evaluation items?

....

....

....

2. How do you think your classroom is doing in relation to those items? What are the classroom strengths and weaknesses?

....

....

3. As a result of undertaking this self-evaluation, what three priority targets would you now set for the coming year (or shorter period)?

1..

2..

3..

4. Are there any further comments or reminders for when you look back on this evaluation?

....

....

....

Date of this evaluation:....................................   Date of next evaluation:..............................

Evaluation carried out by:...

8

Conclusion: Ways Forward

This chapter sums up the thoughts and ideas offered in the book, and suggests some ways forward. It covers:

● the different 'voices' used in discussions about dyslexia

● the journey toward a dyslexia-friendly approach, from backgrounds and definitions, to specifics in classroom practice

● the complicating factors that may interfere with a straightforward development of provision along dyslexia-friendly lines

● the opportunity for optimism as understanding of dyslexia, and understanding of disability, continue to develop.

An examination of dyslexia today reveals that it is discussed in many different 'voices'. There is a dialogue about measurement, test scores and discrepancies, another about neurological linkages; a dialogue about genetics and another about cognitive processing. There is expression in terms of deficit and its antithesis in the disability rights view. There is a socially mediated, broad, everyday understanding that portrays dyslexia as an inability to gain necessary literacy skills in the face of other apparent abilities. Contrasted with this is the view of dyslexia that focuses on a specialised, detailed, identification of subtypes. Further, understandings about dyslexia may differ between international contexts. Dyslexia remains controversial, with no single definition to which all subscribe, and with some outright critics who repudiate dyslexia as a concept altogether.

What we discuss as dyslexia has different meanings for different people, and depends on the discourse that we use. Nevertheless, there is no doubt that some children experience persistent difficulties in gaining aspects of literacy, and these may be compounded with other learning characteristics that operate against a straightforward literacy acquisition. It would be reflecting a positive ethos to speak of these characteristics, as MacKay (2005) does, as differences. But the social context in which we function demands an increasingly higher literacy level, and it is this social context that makes a difference into a difficulty, and thence into a disability.

In the continuous quest for improvement in the provision of state education in the UK, educational ideas and policies have arrived at a point of change. There are several elements to this, and their impact for children experiencing dyslexia remains to be seen. One change likely to have a direct impact is the development, implementation and dissemination of dyslexia-friendly policies and practices in LAs, schools and classrooms.

The journey of the book

This book has sought to trace the journey toward a dyslexia-friendly approach, from backgrounds and definitions, to specifics in classroom practice. In the process, it has shown that dyslexia-friendly characteristics are related to perceptions and ways of thinking about dyslexia, as much as to practical resources.

Starting with an overview of the understandings of dyslexia today, including its place within a social context, the book shows established aspects of dyslexia practice, positioned in terms of a dyslexia-friendly approach. A description of the development of the BDA dyslexia-friendly initiative shows how this approach is being consolidated and used as a marker of quality, and wider social and cultural considerations are explored. A discussion of the family view leads to an exploration of the LA's role, progressing to school practice and then to classroom practice. Practical materials, including a dyslexia access guide, a dyslexia-friendly lesson plan, and a self-evaluation/audit tool, are provided. It is hoped that the book's mixture of ideas and practical suggestions will help practitioners to sustain a dyslexia-friendly classroom.

Complicating factors

The structuring of the dyslexia-friendly initiative as a nested approach to policy and practice demonstrates the potential for valuable change to aid all learners. Nevertheless, there remain other, complex factors to consider, concerned with how LAs will implement and interpret dyslexia-friendly policy. LAs will expect to reduce the number of their statements of SEN focusing on dyslexia. However, there is no guarantee that money thus saved will be fed back to the schools; it may go toward the cost of managing the dyslexia-friendly process as required by the Quality Mark Standards.

In addition, statements of SEN are more than just providers of extra help; they are contracts guaranteeing that a child's learning needs will be met. They address all the child's learning needs, not only those that are most evident, and they describe in detail what the LA will do and what the school will do to help the child, and how this will be monitored to ensure that a child makes necessary progress. Parents may be reluctant to give up statements, and it will take considerable reassurance for them to feel confident that the LA will help their child sufficiently without this contract in place.

If they have not already done so, LAs may delegate special needs funding to schools to give them greater freedom in making their own dyslexia provision. There are some drawbacks attached to this. Previously, dyslexia provision in the LA may have been arranged through the use of a central support team. When the funding for a service is delegated, this may be done by dismantling the service, so that when schools look for service to buy with their new funds, it is no longer there. Sometimes this can cause a vacuum in service provision.

While there is potential for innovation and value for money in schools' management of their own provision, this can take time to arrange and can add to the management work load accordingly. In addition, the amount of funding delegated might not cover the provision a school wishes to make. A further complicating factor is that an LA may structure its policy around a dyslexia-friendly approach that has implications for funding structures, without all of its schools being equally involved in the process, since only a percentage of the schools need to adopt the approach to enable the Quality Mark to be achieved. This too could create a hiatus.

Next, there is a question of what happens when dyslexia-trained staff members move on. This raises the question of whether the LA will fund further training, or whether it will be considered that there is a limit to how much the LA can put into schools before it seeks to pass that cost over to schools.

Finally, there is the question of whether an LA, having invested in the dyslexia-friendly initiative, will then keep doing so. LAs may feel that there is no need to progress to the further levels of the quality process. Educational initiatives and policies change all the time, and once having put dyslexia-friendly processes in place, LAs may expect the changed ethos to maintain its own momentum. If matters are satisfactory, children's dyslexia needs are met, parents are satisfied, and literacy levels improve, then there may not be a need to follow the formal dyslexia-friendly process. Set against this, however, is the advantage that having the formal BDA dyslexia-friendly Quality Mark will present at the tribunal.

In spite of these provisos and caveats, we may expect to see a useful spread of the dyslexia-friendly approach. The initiative and the Quality Mark process, embodied in its standards, represent a well-thought-out and wide-ranging process that LAs benefit from taking on board. Dyslexia-friendly policy and practice seek to improve education and schooling, not just for pupils experiencing dyslexia, but for children with learning needs generally. In many ways, the standards represent overarching good practice, but they also make a firm claim in the interests of children experiencing dyslexia. Without the support of the Quality Mark structure, however, there is always a risk of dilution of ideals and practices.

A climate of change

Knowledge regarding dyslexia and its discourses continues to change and develop, and is unlikely to settle for a while yet. There was a time when it was argued that children experiencing dyslexia need a qualitatively different kind of teaching from those experiencing other kinds of learning difficulties, and this remains the view of some specialists. However, there are indications that this view is changing, linked to the idiosyncratic nature of learning difficulties among children described as experiencing dyslexia, and to the view that what may be needed is a greater intensification and focus of the learning experience.

The question of possible differences between dyslexia and other reading difficulty is still open to discussion. In addition, the best way of generally teaching children to read is not yet resolved, although much is hoped for from synthetic phonics. A synthetic approach to phonics focuses upon blending, in contrast to the analytic approach, which is concerned with breaking words into their component elements. Skilled practitioners probably do both, but there is no doubt that the synthetic phonics approach is expected to improve children's acquisition of literacy skills. The impact of this change on children with a tendency to dyslexia will need to be explored.

It is likely that, if dyslexia is represented by a range, there will continue to be children who experience particularly intractable difficulties and who will benefit from the continued availability of structured, overlearning programmes, delivered by specialist teachers with a deeper skill knowledge. Traditional forms of dyslexia provision are likely to continue to be needed, in tandem with the dyslexia-friendly approach.

However, much can be achieved by creating a more favourable learning environment for children experiencing dyslexia. This does not refer just to the classroom setting but also to the whole learning environment, and it is important to remember at this stage that the dyslexia-friendly approach embodies a whole-LA, whole-school ethos. This is intended to provide a wide-ranging and supportive framework for the interactions that take place between practitioners and learners. Necessarily, most of these occur in the immediate learning environment of the classroom, through practitioners' work.

Many of the characteristics of a dyslexia-friendly learning setting are based on concepts that primary school practitioners already know about, calling on both their training and their personal experience. To this can now be added a more specific dyslexia-oriented knowledge base, disseminated through the whole-school ethos, through the school development plan, and through in-service training. In this way, the dyslexia-friendly initiative offers potential for practitioners and learners. As Karl Nunkoosing (2000) points out, since disability is socially constructed, so will it change, and perceptions will alter. We can see this process taking place in the learning experience provided for children whom we describe as experiencing dyslexia. The dyslexia-friendly initiative provides a step forward; there is scope for optimism.

References

Augur, J., Briggs, S. and Combley, S. (Eds), 2000, *The Hickey Multisensory Language Course* (3rd edn), London, Whurr Publishers

Ayres, D., 1996, 'Assessment of Intelligence, Cognition, and Metacognition: Reflections, Issues and Recommendations', in G. Reid (Ed.), *Dimensions of Dyslexia*, Volume 1, Edinburgh, Moray House Publications, pp. 81–101

Baker, S., 2006, *The New NASEN A–Z of Reading Resources*, London, David Fulton Publishers

Berninger, V., 2004, 'Brain-Based Assessment and Instructional Intervention', in G. Reid and A. Fawcett (Eds), *Dyslexia in Context: Research, Policy and Practice*, London, Whurr Publishers, pp. 90–119

Blackledge, A., 2000, *Literacy, Power and Social Justice*, Stoke on Trent, Trentham Books

Booth, T., and Ainscow, M., 2002, *Index for Inclusion* (rev. edn), Bristol, Centre for Studies on Inclusive Education (CSIE)

British Dyslexia Association (BDA), 1999, *Achieving Dyslexia-Friendly Schools*, Reading, British Dyslexia Association

British Dyslexia Association (BDA), 2004, *Dyslexia-Friendly Local Education Authorities (LEAs) Quality Mark Initiative, the Dyslexia Friendly Standards*, Reading, British Dyslexia Association

British Psychological Society, 1999, *Dyslexia, Literacy and Psychological Assessment*, Report by a Working Party of the Division of Education of the British Psychological Society, Leicester, British Psychological Society

Brooks, G. and National Foundation for Educational Research, 2002, *What Works for Children with Literacy Difficulties? The Effectiveness of Intervention Schemes*, Research Report 380, Annesley, Department for Education and Skills

Connors, C. and Stalker, K., 2003, *The Views and Experiences of Disabled Children and Their Siblings, A Positive Outlook*, London, Jessica Kingsley Publishers

Cowling, H., 2000, *The Word Wasp*, Leeds, Wasp Publications

Cowling, H., 2002, *The Hornet Literacy Primer*, Leeds, Wasp Publications

Cowling, K. and Cowling, H., 1993, *Toe by Toe, Multisensory Manual for Teachers and Parents*, Bradford, Toe by Toe

Cyhlarova, E., Kinsey, K., Hansen, P., Stein, J. and Richardson, A., 2004, *Fatty Acid Status and Visual Function in Adults with Dyslexia*, Paper presented to the 6th British Dyslexia Association Conference, University of Warwick (Abstract)

Davis, R., and Braun, E., 1997, *The Gift of Dyslexia*, London, Souvenir Press

DES (Department of Education and Science), 1978, *Special Educational Needs*: Report of the Committee of Enquiry into the Education of Handicapped Children and Young People (the Warnock Report), London: HMSO

Department for Education (DfE), 1994, *Code of Practice on the Identification and Assessment of Special Educational Needs*, London, HMSO

Department for Education and Skills (DfES), 2001, *Special Educational Needs Code of Practice*, Annesley, DfES Publications

Department for Education and Skills (DfES), 2004, *Removing Barriers to Achievement, the Government's Strategy for SEN*, Annesley, DfES Publications

Department for Education and Skills (DfES) 2005, *Learning and Teaching for Dyslexic Children*, CD-ROM, Annesley, DfES Publications

Dyslexia Action, 2006, *Specific Learning Difficulties*, Information and Addresses SpLD Resources Booklet available at www.dyslexia.org.uk/docs/SPLD_NationalResource06.pdf

Farrell, M., 2001, *Standards and Special Educational Needs*, London, Continuum

Farrell, M., 2004, *Special Educational Needs, A Resource for Practitioners*, London, Paul Chapman Publishers

Fawcett , A., 2001, 'Inclusion – A Parent's Perspective', in L. Peer and G. Reid (Eds), *Dyslexia – Successful Inclusion in the Secondary School*, London, David Fulton Publishers, in association with the British Dyslexia Association, pp. 267–274

Fawcett, A., 2002, 'Dyslexia: A Parent's Perspective', in M. Johnson and L. Peer, (Eds), *The Dyslexia Handbook 2002*, Reading, British Dyslexia Association, pp. 144–148

Frederickson, N. and Cline, T., 2002, *Special Educational Needs, Inclusion and Diversity*, Buckingham, Open University Press

Griffiths, C., Norwich, B. and Burden, B., 2004, 'Parental Agency, Identity and Knowledge: Mothers of Children with Dyslexia', *Oxford Review of Education*, 30 (2), pp. 417–433

Hillier, Y., 2002, *Reflective Teaching in Further and Adult Education*, London, Continuum

Hornsby, B. and Shear, F., 1999, *Alpha to Omega* (5th edn), Oxford, Heinemann

House of Commons Education and Skills Committee, 2006, *Special Educational Needs* (Third Report of Session 2005–06), London, Stationery Office.

Johnson, M., 2004, *Pupils' Views of Dyslexia-Friendly Teaching*, PowerPoint presentation to the 6th International Conference of the British Dyslexia Association, Warwick University, 2005

Johnson, M. and Peer, L. (Eds), 2002, *The Dyslexia Handbook 2002*, Reading, British Dyslexia Association, pp. 229–233

Johnson, M., Phillips, S. and Peer, L. 1999, *Multisensory Teaching System for Reading*, Manchester, Manchester Metropolitan University

Kelly, K., 2002, 'Dyslexia and Bilingual Pupils', in M. Johnson and L. Peer (Eds), *The Dyslexia Handbook 2002*, Reading, British Dyslexia Association, pp. 229–233

Landon, J., 2001, 'Inclusion and Dyslexia – the Exclusion of Bilingual Learners?', in L. Peer and G. Reid (Eds), *Dyslexia – Successful Inclusion in the Secondary School*, London, David Fulton Publishers, published in association with British Dyslexia Association, pp. 182–187

Lloyd, S. and Berthelot, C., 1992, *Self-Empowerment: How to Get What You Want from Life*, London, Kogan Page

MacKay, N., 2001, *Achieving the Dyslexia-Friendly School – The Hawarden Approach*, Paper presented to the 5th BDA International Conference, available online at:
http://www.bdainternationalconference-org/2001/presentations/

MacKay, N., 2005, *Removing Dyslexia as a Barrier to Achievement*, Wakefield, SEN Marketing

MacKay, N., 2006, 'Evaluating the BDA Quality Mark for LEAs', in S. Tresman and A. Cooke (Eds), *The Dyslexia Handbook 2006*, Reading, British Dyslexia Association, pp. 298–302

Marsh, A., 2002, *Resourcing Additional and Special Educational Needs in England 10 Years on (1992–2002)*, Education Management Information Exchange (EMIE) Report No. 66, Slough, National Foundation for Educational Research (NFER)

McKeown, S., 1999, *Dyslexia and ICT – Building on Success*, Coventry, British Educational Communication and Technology Agency (BECTA)

Miles, E., 1989, *The Bangor Dyslexia Teaching System*, London, Whurr Publishers

Morgan, N., 2000, *Paired or Shared Reading*, Child Literacy Centre, available online at: http://childliteracy.com/paired.html

Morton, J. and Frith, U., 1995, 'Causal Modelling: A Structural Approach to Developmental Pathology', in D. Cicchetti and D. Cohen (Eds), *Manual of Developmental Psychopathology*, New York, Wiley

Moseley, D., 1995, *ACE Spelling Dictionary* (2nd edition), Wisbech, LDA

Murphy, K., 1992, 'Parental Perceptions of the Professionals Involved with Children with Special Educational Needs', in G. Vulliamy and R. Webb (Eds), *Teacher Research and Special Educational Needs*, London, David Fulton Publishers, pp. 105–122

National Assembly for Wales, 2002, *Special Educational Needs Code of Practice for Wales*, Cardiff, National Assembly for Wales

Nunkoosing, K., 2000, 'Constructing Learning Disability', *Journal of Learning Disabilities*, 4 (1), pp.49–62

O'Brien, C., 2006, 'Dyslexia-Friendly Schools Scheme in Liverpool', in S. Tresman, and A. Cooke (Eds), *The Dyslexia Handbook 2006*, Reading, British Dyslexia Association, pp. 293–297

Paradice, R., 2001, 'An Investigation into the Social Construction of Dyslexia', *Educational Psychology in Practice*, 17,3, pp. 214–225

Peer, L. and Reid, G., (Eds), 2001, *Dyslexia – Successful Inclusion in the Secondary School*, London, David Fulton Publishers, published in association with British Dyslexia Association

Qualifications, Curriculum and Assessment Authority for Wales (ACCAC), 2002, *A Focus on Achievement – Guidance on Including Pupils with Additional Needs in Whole School Target Setting*, Birmingham, ACCAC Publications

Qualifications and Curriculum Authority (QCA), 2004, *More than Words; Multimodal Texts in the Classroom*, Sudbury, QCA Publications

Rack, J., 2004, 'The Theory and Practice of Specialist Literacy Teaching', in G. Reid and A. Fawcett (Eds), *Dyslexia in Context: Research, Policy and Practice*, London, Whurr Publishers, pp. 120–31

Reid, G., (Ed.), 1996, *Dimensions of Dyslexia*, Vol. 1, Edinburgh, Moray House Publications

Reid, G. 2002, 'Definitions of Dyslexia', in M. Johnson and L. Peer. (Eds), *The Dyslexia Handbook 2002*, Reading, British Dyslexia Association

Reid, G., 2003, *Dyslexia, A Practitioner's Handbook*, (3rd edn), Chichester, Wiley.

Reid. G. 2005a, *Dyslexia and Inclusion*, London, David Fulton Publishers in association with the National Association for Special Educational Needs (NASEN)

Reid, G., 2005b, 'Dyslexia', in A. Lewis and B. Norwich (Eds), *Special Teaching for Special Children?*, Maidenhead, Open University Press

Reid, G. 2005c, *Dyslexia*, London, Continuum International Publishing Group

Reid, G., and Fawcett, A., 2004, 'An Overview of Developments in Dyslexia', in G. Reid and A. Fawcett (Eds), *Dyslexia in Context: Research, Policy and Practice*, London, Whurr Publishers, pp. 3–19

Reid Lyon, G. Shaywitz, S., Chhabra, V. and Sweet, R., 2004, 'Evidence-Based Reading Policy in the U.S.', in G. Reid, G and A. Fawcett (Eds), *Dyslexia in Context: Research, Policy and Practice*, London, Whurr Publishers, pp. 161–176

Richardson, A., Cyhlarova, E., Montgomery, P., Lowerson, S. and Portwood, M., 2004, *Treatment with Omega-3 and Omega-6 Fatty Acids Can Improve Reading and Spelling Progress in Children with Developmental Coordination Disorder: A Randomised Controlled Trial*, Paper presented to the 6th British Dyslexia Association Conference, University of Warwick (Abstract)

Riddick, B., 1996, *Living with Dyslexia, The Social and Emotional Consequences of Specific Learning Difficulties*, London, Routledge

Riddick, B., 2001, 'Dyslexia and Inclusion: Time for a Social Model Perspective?', *International Studies in Sociology of Education*, 11(3), pp 223–236

Riddick, B., Wolfe, J. and Lumsdon, D., 2002, *Dyslexia, a Practical Guide for Teachers and Parents*, London, David Fulton Publishers

Roberts, H., 2001, 'Acknowledging Need', *A Survey of Welsh Medium and Bilingual Provision for Pupils with Special Educational Needs in Wales*, Cardiff, Welsh Language Board

Scott, R., 2003, 'A Counsellor's Perspective on Dyslexia', in M. Thomson (Ed.) *Dyslexia Included, A Whole School Approach*, London, David Fulton Publishers, pp. 82–92

Smith, D., 2000, 'The National Literacy Strategy and Pupils with Dyslexia', in D. Smith (Ed.), *Success in the Literacy Hour*, Tamworth, NASEN, pp. 85–88

Snowling, M., 2002, *Dyslexia* (2nd edn), Oxford, Blackwell

Stein, J., 2004, 'Dyslexia Genetics', in G. Reid and A. Fawcett (Eds), *Dyslexia in Context: Research, Policy and Practice*, London, Whurr Publishers, pp. 76–89

Stone, C., (1998) *Beat Dyslexia* Wisbech, Learning Development Aids

Stone, C. Franks, E., Nicholson, M. and Schofield, M.,1998, *Beat Dyslexia Activity Packs*, (Books 1–6) Wisbech, LDA.

Thomas, G. and Loxley, A., 2001, *Deconstructing Special Educational Needs and Constructing Inclusion*, Buckingham, Open University Press

Tomlinson, S., 2001, *Education in a Post-Welfare Society*, Buckingham, Open University Press

Thomson, M.,1985, *Developmental Dyslexia* (2nd edn), London, Cole and Whurr.

Tolmie, A., 2006, 'Secrets of Dyslexia Unlocked', *The Scotsman*, 27 Nov

Werquin, P., 2006, *Words Count*, Paris, Organization for Economic Cooperation and Development available online at: http://www.oecdobserver.org/news/

Woods, K., 1998, 'Dyslexia, Questions from a Social Psychology Perspective', *Educational Psychology in Practice*, 13 (4), pp. 274–277

Index